ECONOMIES OF SCALE IN HIGHER EDUCATION

Most people think a successful city has to be big: but even so they are not clear what counts as big. They tend to judge by a count of heads, but really it is a matter of effectiveness. If we do count heads we must be careful how we do it: we should include only citizens, not slaves etc. There is a difference between a big city and a great one.

A city that is too big collapses as a community. The essential criterion is that the citizens should know each other as individuals: otherwise it would be impossible to administer justice or to hold elections for office. (Aristotle *Politics* VII.4)

Contributed by John Dancy, Conference Chairman

ECONOMIES
OF SCALE
IN HIGHER EDUCATION

Edited for the Higher Education Foundation
by
SINCLAIR GOODLAD

SOCIETY FOR RESEARCH INTO HIGHER EDUCATION

Research into Higher Education Monographs

The Society for Research into Higher Education
At the University, Guildford, Surrey GU2 5XH

First published 1983

© 1983 The Society for Research into Higher Education

ISBN 0 946376 00 X

Printed in England by Direct Design (Bournemouth) Ltd. Printers,
Butts Pond Industrial Estate, Sturminster Newton,
Dorset DT10 1AZ

CONTENTS

CONTENTS

PREFACE AND ACKNOWLEDGEMENTS

This book is the outcome of a conference sponsored jointly by the Higher Education Foundation and the Department of Education and Science (DES). The planning of the conference was undertaken by Pauline Perry, Jonathan May, and Sinclair Goodlad, assisted at various stages by John Dancy, Kevin Keohane, Christian Schumacher, and John Gay. The detailed organization of the conference (booking of accommodation, duplicating and circulating of papers, etc.) was carried out by Mrs. Ann King, Pauline Perry's assistant at the DES, to whom the Trustees of the Foundation are profoundly grateful.

The Trustees of the Foundation (listed at Appendix C) are also grateful to the authors of the papers here printed, and to the following who presented papers which greatly enriched the conference discussion but which, for lack of space, have not been reprinted — Edwin Kerr, Geoffrey Nokes, Angela Cooper, and Maureen Sweetman of the CNAA on 'The Changing Role of Monotechnic Institutions';* Eric Briault on 'The Balance of Criteria Used in Deciding the Appropriate Size of Secondary Schools'; Cedric Cullingford on 'Some Effects of Merging Institutions into Polytechnics'; and John Wyatt and John Gay on 'The Educational Effects of Different Sizes and Types of Academic Organization'. All who took part in the conference (Appendix B) helped to refine, by criticism and discussion, the ideas discussed in this book, in particular Tony Becher, Maurice Kogan, and David Harrison who acted as rapporteurs of the discussion groups. Any clarity apparent in the review of the conference owes much to their distillation of the collective wisdom of the participants; I must, however, claim final responsibility for what is written in chapter 9.

The views expressed in the chapters are those of the authors: they do not necessarily represent the views either of the Trustees of the Higher Education Foundation or of the DES.

The Trustees of the Higher Education Foundation are grateful for benefactions which, in addition to the funding provided by the DES, made possible the conference on which this book is based, notably those of the St. Luke's College Trust, an anonymous Roman Catholic benefactor, and the

---

*The CNAA possesses a rich resource of archive material concerning the effects on diversification of studies in higher education stemming from the mergers and amalgamations of colleges discussed in this paper. *Bona fide* scholars studying higher education who wish to consult this material are invited to apply direct to D. Kerr at the CNAA.

Sony Corporation (recording equipment).

Finally, as editor I acknowledge gratefully the help of Gerald Collier, who acted as the SRHE agent in the publication of the book and, together with Sally Kington, the SRHE Publications Officer, did the house editing.

Sinclair Goodlad
Imperial College
May 1983

INTRODUCTION

Sinclair Goodlad

This book examines the concept of Economies of Scale as applied to institutions of higher education from Economic, Educational, Administrative, Sociological, Psychological, and Political perspectives. Its aim is to throw light on what combination of factors concerning the size of institutions and of units within institutions should inform policy and practice.

GENESIS OF THE BOOK

The book is the outcome of a conference jointly sponsored by the Higher Education Foundation and the Department of Education and Science in October 1982. A brief description of the background to the initiative will indicate why the book takes its present form.

The Higher Education Foundation is an independent educational trust (Registered Charity number 281719) formed in 1980 by the merging of the Foundation for the Study of Values in Higher Education and the long-established Higher Education Group (formerly the University Teachers' Group). The purpose of the Foundation is to analyse and develop a greater understanding of the various underlying objectives of higher and further education, both direct and indirect, the philosophical basis of such objectives, and the methods whereby such objectives may be pursued.

The Foundation is not concerned with propaganda for a preconceived theory or belief; its concern is to illuminate areas of choice in the field of higher and further education for the benefit of the public, and in particular for the benefit of students and teachers.

The Trustees of the Foundation, acting as a study group, will be seeking over a number of years to work out a coherent theory of higher education which they hope will constitute a more reliable long-term guide to individual and institutional action than the often merely expedient financial, demographic, and other administrative concerns which currently inform policy. Such a theory of higher education will only be achieved if current assumptions about all aspects of education — curriculum, teaching methods, collegial structures, and so on — are submitted to regular and radical scrutiny designed to illuminate the underlying assumptions operating in specific cases.

Most questions concerning education are ultimately political questions, not least because they frequently involve issues concerning the distribution of money and power. Because they are political questions, they involve philosophical questions onto which must be brought to bear not just the formal apparatus of commentating disciplines (such as academic philosophy, sociology, and theology), but the full range of perceptions (moral, spiritual, aesthetic) implied in or constituting religions and ideologies — in short, styles and systems of thought which deal with fundamental questions of meaning in human affairs. It is with this level of analysis of issues in higher education that the Higher Education Foundation is primarily concerned. The Trustees believe, however, that these broader questions are best approached obliquely. Rather than trying to impose on the world as it is experienced institutionally some great preconstructed system of thought, the Trustees are seeking to work interactively — that is, by addressing current issues in higher education which bristle with value questions, and thereby trying to extract those questions which merit further clarification. For this reason, the Foundation has begun its work by arranging a series of small conferences or consultations (Appendix D).

Each of the Foundation's consultations is designed to achieve some statement of:

a   what needs to be known for issues to be further clarified (an *agenda for research*);

b   what in the long term ought to be done in practice in the light of what is already known and what it is anticipated that research will reveal (the articulation of some sort of consensual *philosophical position* on the subject or, if disagreements are profound, the identification of the main areas of dispute);

c   what can be done in the short term to adjust current practice to what seems, in the light of the philosophical position arrived at, to be desirable (proposals for *individual and institutional action*).

The intention is that each consultation will result in suggestions of future work which should be undertaken by the Foundation itself and by others concerned with the study of higher education and, perhaps more importantly, of options open to practitioners in each area studied.

The planning group of the Higher Education Foundation (later to become its Trustees) spent much time discussing the concept of 'collegiality' — what conditions fostered or inhibited it, whether it aided or impeded the academic and personal development of students, and so on. What was abundantly clear was that the reorganization of teacher training in the 1970s had brought about a significant loss of institutional identity for small monotechnic institutions which had been absorbed into larger institutions (polytechnics or institutes of higher education or, less frequently, universities), and that considerable organizational and community problems were emerging from split-site arrangements.

The thinking of the Trustees was focused by a discussion paper by Dr. Jonathan May, Director of Derby Lonsdale College of Higher Education, who suggested that the concept of 'Economies of scale in higher education' involved many of the issues with which the Trustees were concerned. The movement in the 1970s from small monotechnic institutions to larger, more complex ones was officially justified, he suggested, by the assertion that such a move would lead to economies of scale. The optimistic expectations were, *inter alia*:

— that larger institutions would be more cost effective in terms of overall unit costs and that there would be many specific savings because of the sharing of resources;
— that academic units clustered together would more easily be able to justify the acquisition of specialist resources, say library, reprographic, and suchlike services, and to operate these economically;
— that large institutions would make a range of courses available locally to more part-time students and students would be able to attend full-time higher education from their home bases (with implicit savings in such arrangements);
— that there would be greater flexibility in planning and executing a wider range of courses, for example permitting larger institutions to withstand and cushion fluctuations in the supply and demand for school teachers and cope with the consequent diversification in the use of resources;
— that the academic stewardship of the larger institution would be more responsible, for example, by establishing, monitoring, and validating higher standards more effectively than could small institutions.

By September 1980, when the planning group of the Foundation was considering these matters, there were significant indications that some of the social, psychological, and administrative costs of mergers and amalgamations were making the financial benefits (even where these could be clearly identified) somewhat difficult to justify. Since then, the McNamara and Ross report (1982) *The B.Ed. Degree and Its Future* has confirmed the existence of widespread unease about these matters:

There have been no significant gains in resources in the opinion of staff and students. There is no evidence that amalgamations lead to an increase in the range of courses available. There may be *less* opportunity for B.Ed. students to meet students studying for other qualifications ... and, even when students are mixed, there is little evidence that friendships emerge across course divisions. Multi-site operations would appear to cause problems of course coherence and travel between sites, and the value of such operations must be questioned except in those cases where the two sites are physically close. There are, no doubt, important logistical and administrative arguments for amalgamating institutions providing roughly the same programmes; caution has to be exercised in adducing academic, social and cultural arguments in support of these policy decisions (p.34).

In July 1981, the University Grants Committee (UGC) announced widespread cuts in funding to universities. In this sector of higher education, too, there are somewhat obscure notions about optimum size of institutions, the 'viability' of departments, and the costs and benefits of mergers. That notions of optimum size do inform planning decisions is witnessed by the fact that the new universities established in the early 1960s were given target figures for their student numbers. It seemed clear, however, that the rationale for proposing institutions, or departments, of specific sizes had fallen into disrepair.

The Trustees of the Higher Education Foundation therefore approached the DES with a proposal for a jointly sponsored consultation on the theme of 'Economies of scale in higher education'. Through the good offices of Mrs. Pauline Perry, HMI, this was arranged. The plan was to solicit a number of papers on various aspects of the issue and subject them to critical scrutiny by an invited gathering representing the DES, universities, polytechnics, institutes of higher education, and LEA school administration (where similar problems had been experienced in deciding upon the size of schools), and individual scholars (from the United States as well as the United Kingdom) who had studied aspects of the sociology, psychology, and economics of higher education. Following the consultation, papers have been revised and an analytical review of issues has been undertaken (see chapter 9).

THE ARRANGEMENT OF THE CHAPTERS

The book begins with a review of the economic arguments for economies of scale in higher education (chapters 2 and 3); continues with analysis of some of the educational and administrative benefits hoped for from particular sizes and types of institution, with some analysis of the extent to which these have or have not been achieved (chapters 4 and 5); moves on to a review of some of the sociological and psychological effects of institutions of different sizes (chapter 6); and offers (chapter 7) an attempt to synthesize all the major organizational factors into a proposal for an optimally-sized university. Chapter 8 illustrates the relationship of the concept of economies of scale to the issues being considered by the National Advisory Body for Local Authority Higher Education (NAB). The last chapter (9) reviews some of the major issues identified at the HEF/DES conference, suggests topics for future research, and examines some factors (arising from both the papers and the discussion at the conference) which should influence long-term planning of the provision of higher education.

In chapter 2, Kevin Sear examines the application of the concept of economies of scale to costs in higher education, raising some of the key policy questions such as: What is the appropriate level of funding required for different student populations at any given standard of provision? How many institutions of higher education does this consideration argue? What is the minimum size desirable for an institution, academic department, or individual course? To what extent should institutions specialize, whether in particular subjects or in teaching rather than research? He examines some of the factors contributing to economies of scale at each institutional level, citing evidence that average costs fall indefinitely as student numbers rise. No one, however, believes that purely financial arguments should be carried to their logical conclusion: it is necessary to incorporate other factors in the argument.

Can cost-benefit analysis, therefore, be applied to the concept of economies of scale in higher education? In chapter 3, Mark Blaug answers that question with an unambiguous 'yes'. He knows, however, no way of *quantifying* the educational and psychological advantages of small size. The burden of proof, he argues, is on the critics of cost-benefit analysis; unless they can place *numbers* on the educational value of being small, the financial case for larger higher education institutions will carry the day.

There are, however, many arguments concerning the appropriate size of educational institutions and departments which, although not capable of precise quantification, can nevertheless be stated with sufficient force and clarity to influence policy and practice. The ensuing chapters seek to illustrate these.

As new pressures appear to build up in favour of institutional mergers, it is instructive to examine what have been some of the effects of those recently undertaken. Gordon Wheeler's examination (chapter 4) of 'Some Effects of Merging Small Further Education Institutions into Larger Ones' laments the apparent lack of any central record of mergers undertaken in the last decade, of the reasons for them, or of their effects. He offers an analytical review of some of the main reasons for the merging of institutions and of some of the factors inhibiting mergers. He then reviews some of the effects of mergers, drawing upon extensive interviews with staff, and suggests important lessons for future mergers. He concludes with a chronicle of the positive and negative effects of a specific merger.

Gordon Wheeler's material is very valuable in illuminating the *process* of merger. There remains, however, the issue of the long-term consequences of size once institutions have settled down.

Martin Trow argues (in chapter 5) for the benefits of very large institutions, provided that they are loosely articulated internally. By examining examples of cooperation between autonomous institutions, he shows how the effective size of institutions can be far greater than their nominal size. Flexibility of funding and permeability of institutional boundaries can produce structures which combine the virtues of smallness and academic coherence with the freedom of action of large organizations.

Russell Thomas and Arthur Chickering, in chapter 6, review much of the literature on 'Institutional Size, Higher Education, and Student Development'. They present very strong social and psychological arguments in favour of small institutions (in marked contrast to the purely financial cost arguments of chapter 2 and 3 in favour of larger ones).

Interestingly, although much research literature advocates largeness or smallness (according to which disciplinary perspective is adopted), few writers commit themselves to a specific optimum size for an institution. This deficiency is provocatively remedied by Christian Schumacher in chapter 7 on 'The Problem of Scale in Higher Education'. Drawing upon extensive experience of restructuring industrial organizations and applying the insights to the study of academic ones, Schumacher shows how economies at any one of seven organizational levels can produce diseconomies at other levels. His summary table (7.1, page 64) illustrating 'Economies and Diseconomies of Scale' is a powerful synthesis of economic, sociological, and psychological analyses. He concludes by arguing that an optimum sized university should contain between twelve and twenty departments and thus a total of between about 1,500 and 4,000 students.

Christopher Ball, in chapter 8, shows how educational planners, operating under severe pressures of time and finance, rank various criteria (including that of economies of scale) in order of priority. His paper is a timely reminder that educational research and reflection can probably only bear fruit over a longish time span. It is also historically important, as a record of how an influential committee conceived of its task at a formative stage of its thought. The final chapter 9 reviews some of the issues, possibilities for research, and factors which could usefully inform long-term planning of higher education.

ECONOMIES OF SCALE IN HIGHER EDUCATION

Kevin Sear

This chapter discusses the application of the concept of economies of scale to costs in higher education. The *Dictionary of Economic Terms* defines 'economies of scale' as 'the gains by way of reduced costs of production per unit of output often arising from increasing the size of a plant, business or industry'. The concept has been developed in application to industry, where the scale of operations can have a critical effect on costs, profits, and even the viability of a plant, firm, or, particularly at a national level, an entire industry. Indeed, economies of scale have often been used as a justification for nationalization, either because this was the only way to secure large cost savings while avoiding undesirable private monopoly, or because this was the only way to make the home-based producers competitive with large-scale enterprises overseas. This is not to say, however, that in the event the economies hoped for have always been achieved.

Within the framework of assumptions on which the theory is based, the idea of economies of scale can be applied to any resource-using activity. This includes the social services, not least education, despite the fact that these are generally funded by the Government, do not sell their output and are not concerned with questions of profitability or competitiveness. Perhaps the most important assumption in the context of this paper is that it is possible to consider the scale of an activity as it affects costs, without any important side-effects on the quality or general characteristics of what is produced. Given this assumption, the cost analysis can be dignified by the title 'economies of scale', with its rather approving flavour, because on this basis a reduction in cost really implies an increase in value for money. However, much of this book is concerned with whether such an assumption can reasonably be made for higher education, and the use of the term 'economies of scale' in this chapter is certainly not intended to pre-judge the issue.

Any potential for economies of scale is clearly very important for education in view of the large sums of public money involved and the need to ensure that it is spent as effectively as possible. There are in fact a number of important policy issues (for consideration at various levels, eg central Government, the UGC and NAB, individual institutions and departments within institutions) which might be influenced by an appreciation of the existence of or potential for economies of scale. These include:

a   What is the appropriate level of funding required for different student populations at any given standard of provision? (Or — to put this in a form more consistent with the apparent requirements of the present financial regime — what combination of student numbers and quality of provision can be afforded for any given level of available funds?)

b   For how many institutions of higher education does this consideration argue?

c   What is the minimum size desirable for an institution, academic department or individual course?

d   To what extent should institutions specialize whether in particular subjects or in teaching rather than research (or vice versa)?

To repeat, it would, of course, be wrong to suggest that such issues can be wholly determined by reference to costs and indeed there are many factors which affect costs apart from scale. Nevertheless, a knowledge of the relationship between scale and unit costs would clearly be of great value. It might be thought that this is not the ideal time to be considering economies of scale, faced as we are with a system which is currently contracting, and the future size of which is uncertain. The heyday of studies of scale effects in higher education was in the late 60s and early 70s when we were looking to a period of rapid expansion, though the economies achieved in practice during this period were sometimes disappointing. However, in some ways, an appreciation of scale economies is just as important today. Contraction might occur in a way which led either to large increases in unit costs or to lower standards of provision as overheads ate up an increasing proportion of total expenditure. This would be highly undesirable if such effects could be avoided by a more efficient management of resources. It is most important that, within the constraints imposed by the existence of buildings with a more or less substantial remaining life-span, and of staff with a greater or lesser degree of tenure, contraction should be planned in such a way as to maximize value for money, and that such implications of the pursuit of value for money as the closure of courses, departments or institutions should be faced.

In this context, it is important to draw a distinction between the long term and the short term. Economists define these time horizons in terms of the extent to which the various inputs of production can be varied. The factor of production which is usually most difficult to vary in the short run is physical capacity in terms of laboratories, classrooms, libraries, etc. There are almost always short-run economies of scale involved in maximizing the utilization of existing capacity since much expenditure is related more to the size and age and type of capacity than to the extent to which that capacity is used. Unit costs (either of students or research) will, therefore, tend to fall as utilization is increased. This, however, is very different from the proposition that large institutions are more cost-effective than small ones when both are operating at full capacity. The latter situation would imply long-run economies of scale and would have implications for future planning as new buildings were required to cater for expansion or replacement of older buildings, or as decisions were required about the optimal pattern of contraction. Sometimes there can be conflict between short-run and long-run optimization. For example, it takes time to close an institution and during that time it will be operating in what appears to be an inefficient way from a viewpoint of short-run cost minimization. This short-term inefficiency can perhaps be justified by reference to the longer term benefits of rationalization.

FACTORS AFFECTING ECONOMIES OF SCALE

Economies of scale may occur at different hierarchical levels as indicated by the reference in the definition quoted in para. 1 to 'plant, business or industry'. In higher education the most important distinction is probably that between economies in central expenditure and economies in departmental expenditure. The latter will depend almost entirely on the size of individual departments and courses. Economies of scale in central expenditure (the most important components of which will be administration, repair and maintenance expenditure, and libraries) will depend partly on the overall size of the institution but also on the extent of specialization and economies of scale realized by departments. The latter is most clearly true in the case of libraries, where the effect on expenditure of an increase in student numbers will clearly differ according to whether the expansion occurs in existing subject areas or whether new departments are being set up. It may, however, also be true, to some extent, of administrative costs. If, for example, administrative expenditure is affected by the number of staff as well as by the number of students; then an expansion of student numbers which results in a lower ratio of staff to students will increase administrative costs by less than an expansion of student numbers which calls forth a proportionate increase in staff.

As noted above, economies of scale in repairs and maintenance and other building-related costs may differ greatly as between the short term and the long term. In the short term the scope for economies will depend mainly on the extent to which existing buildings, equipment and staff are used to their full capacity. In the case of buildings, for example, this will be related to the extent to which class sizes match the size of rooms available and to the proportion of available room-hours actually used. It should not be assumed that it would be feasible, let alone optimal, to use all the rooms to the maximum of capacity. Some spare rooms will always be needed for the sake of flexibility while, particularly in the case of laboratories, preparation time will cut down the amount of time available for teaching or research purposes. On the other hand, existing capacity is not independent of the way courses are organized. It is for example, possible to envisage courses being arranged so as to make it possible to use classrooms for a higher proportion of the week, or for a greater number of weeks per year. None of this presupposes that building-related expenditure will be unaffected by intensity of use; it does, however, seem reasonable to suppose that such costs as repairs, maintenance, and rate of depreciation, will not rise *proportionately* as use increases.

In the longer term the question is whether, used to full capacity, larger buildings are cheaper than smaller ones. In fact, economies of this kind are more likely to be determined by economies elsewhere. So, for example, if large institutions economize on staff, administrative, or library costs, there are also likely to be savings in unit premises costs simply because staff, administrators and libraries also require building space.

Turning now to departmental costs, what will be the main determinants of economies of scale here? A number of key factors can be isolated:

a   the structure of courses in terms of the balance between lectures, seminars and tutorials;
b   the maximum viable sizes of groups to be taught;
c   the number of options available on the course;
d   the ratio of teaching to research time for academic staff.

The basic structure of a course will generally be determined in the first instance by considerations of what is optimal from an educational viewpoint. But the more that courses can be concentrated into lectures and the larger the maximum size of group the greater the scope for economies of scale. In theory, for a lecture with no student participation there should be no limit to the allowable class size; this is what underlies the economies of scale of the Open University, though in conventional institutions the maximum size will, in practice, be determined by the size of available lecture rooms.

A related point here is that, as the number of students on a course rises, the time spent on course preparation does not need to rise proportionately. To the extent that it does rise, the extra effort can go into preparing an improved course. The Open University is a classic example, since one of its most distinctive features is that the large numbers of students taking each course have allowed substantial effort and collaboration between academics in the preparation of high quality course materials and presentation. The same principle could be applied in the mainstream system of higher education, albeit on a smaller scale. In fact, widening the point somewhat, it is quite possible that there are economies of scale in preparation time which could be tapped by greater collaboration not only between lecturers but between institutions. This should be especially possible in the case of first year material in many courses where the present rule is that each lecturer prepares his own course even though the content may not change rapidly over time and even though much the same basic material is being covered in very similar courses all over the country. There are no doubt some arguments to be considered against collaboration but, if capitalizing on expertise in this way can give rise to savings and/or improved quality, then this possibility is worthy of further exploration — possibly building on the work which has already been done by the Lumsden development project at Heriot-Watt University (Lumsden 1978).

The relationship between economies of scale and the number of options is a tricky one. Clearly, for any given number of students, the more options offered, the smaller is the average group size, the more time is necessary for preparation, and the higher is the average teaching cost. In theory this need not necessarily lead to a rise in the minimum attainable average cost: it might simply mean that a larger total enrolment was necessary in order to secure it. In practice, the minimum probably would rise because large lectures are likely to be used less often for options than for the main course. It is sometimes suggested that there is a correlation between the number of enrolments and the number of options offered. To the extent that this is true it would mean that the benefits of scale economies were being used to extend options rather than to secure savings. This is not necessarily a bad thing and a wide range of options may be considered educationally desirable. What is important is that the costs involved should not go unrecognized.

The interaction between research and economies of scale is complex and largely unexplored. The previous two paragraphs have considered the factors affecting the relationship between student numbers and teaching-related lecturer time. If, as numbers expand, the ratio of the latter to total lecturer time remains constant, then there will be no further economies. This, however, implies that the quantity of research time would vary in proportion to teaching time, and, in practice, this might well happen if all academics were expected to devote a certain proportion of their time to research. Whether they should do so, however, is questionable. An argument could be put forward to the effect that there is a national need for research which is unrelated to the number of students requiring tuition or to the quality of teaching provision. On this logic, marginal students should have no effect on the quantity of research being done with the result that, as student numbers expanded, overall unit costs could fall on this account. Strictly speaking, this would not be an example of economies of scale since the reduction in unit costs would really be due to a change in the balance of outputs, as would be made clear by an appropriate attribution of costs. In practice, however, much public policy focuses on overall unit costs per student (referred to in some contexts as 'the unit of resource'), and from this viewpoint, the effect would appear as an economy of scale. What is important to note is that it would be an economy related to the national total of student numbers and could not be taken to apply at an individual institution. Unlike the other economies, therefore, there would be no savings under this head from simply concentrating a given number of students in a smaller number of institutions or departments. Indeed, one implication of this argument is that, if the total quantity of research (rather than research per lecturer) were required to remain constant, then, in a time of contraction, this would create an unavoidable upward pressure on overall unit costs.

One issue which is important here is the interrelationship between teaching and research. A defence sometimes raised for the constant ratio of teaching to research time is that the two are in the nature of 'joint products', such that time spent on research has a beneficial effect on the quality of teaching. The latter would suffer if a substantial proportion of teachers did no research. There are a number of counter-arguments to this view. One is that the above does not necessarily imply that any lecturers do no research: it simply means that the *average* amount of time spent on research would fall as student numbers rose. Secondly, it could be argued that even if the quality of teaching were to suffer in the way described, this must be set alongside the costs: it is possible that quality could be maintained more cheaply than by financing research, which might have little intrinsic value. More fundamentally, the whole basis of the argument might be challenged: is there any hard evidence that teaching is favourably affected by research? It is possible that greater benefits could be obtained by specialization which allowed the law of comparative advantage to operate more freely. There may also be economies of scale in research which are missed because individuals or groups are distracted by the demands of teaching. It is difficult to see how such propositions could ever be conclusively tested but it may be useful to quote from a recent paper (Oldham 1982) summarizing a discussion by the Society for Research into Higher Education: 'The generally accepted wisdom in the past has been that the two (teaching and research) are intimately related. This view was challenged at the seminar and most participants agreed that there was no evidence to support this contention. Some studies which have examined the issue have concluded that the reverse may be the case.'

One final point to note about the factors affecting economies of scale in departmental expenditure is that they are all intimately connected with questions of course organization and quality usually regarded as the province of professional educational judgements. While we would argue strongly that consideration of cost should be taken seriously into account, it must be recognized that we are entering areas which could raise sensitive issues of academic autonomy. Therefore, although economies of scale may figure in central funding decisions, difficulties are bound to arise in trying to apply these decisions consistently at local level, since it will never be possible for such factors as the lecture/seminar split, group sizes, or the number of options to be made the subject of strict, centrally determined norms. The problems of how in practice to allocate funds and the related and equally important issue of how to create appropriate *incentives* to achieve economies, are beyond the scope of this chapter but an interesting discussion can be found in Dunworth and Cook (1976).

MEASURING ECONOMIES OF SCALE IN HIGHER EDUCATION
While an understanding of the nature of scale effects and the reasons for them is, in itself, very useful, it is also essential, for planning purposes, to go some way towards measuring their size. In the measurement of costs in

production industries two fundamentally different approaches may be distinguished. The first, which may be dubbed the 'engineering' approach, involves asking those with a technical knowledge of the production processes what costs would be at various hypothetical levels of output as compared with the costs of producing the actual level of output. The second or 'cross-section' approach involves a comparison of the actual costs incurred by firms or plants at different levels of output as observed. There are difficulties with both approaches, particularly where the product itself is varied and difficult to measure, as it is in higher education; both approaches have, nevertheless, been tried with interesting results.

A good example of the engineering approach can be found in a study carried out by a team under Bottomley at Bradford University as part of a wide-ranging exercise on costs and potential economies in higher education undertaken in the early '70s and reported by Bottomley (1976). As part of their project they devised a method of calculating the number and cost of academic staff required to teach a course (taking account of the variables mentioned above). This was used to calculate how teaching costs per student would vary as enrolment expanded, for a number of courses at Bradford. (This was of particular interest at the time because a large increase in intake was anticipated.) The key determinant of costs was the number of teaching meetings required: these tended to rise less than proportionately with the number of students as attendance at lectures increased and as the proportion of 'empty' places at other classes fell.

The teaching cost functions discovered by Bottomley's team varied considerably from subject to subject, mainly because of differences between subjects in the size of teaching groups. Nevertheless, in all the cases examined it was true, first, that unit costs fell as enrolments increased; second, that the rate of decline fell as enrolments increased; and, third, that the decline was punctuated by sharp increases at the enrolment levels at which a series of meetings had to be duplicated. The potential for economies was substantial. It was calculated that an approximate doubling of enrolments (approximate because an exact doubling would not be sensible if it took enrolments just above a point of meeting duplication) would lead to reductions in teaching unit costs of between 18 and 48% with an average reduction of over 30%. This did not require any reduction in the quality of teaching (contact hours and other components of course structure were held constant); nor did it require any rise in average lecturer time devoted to teaching: in fact, by ignoring preparation time, it probably understated the true scope for economies.

Calculations were also done on the potential economies arising from a fuller use of classroom and laboratory space. These included consideration of some radical options involving an extension of the working week and a double intake of students each year (having the effect of bringing space into use for a much higher proportion of the total time available). There were problems because it was not easy to assess what the maximum feasible capacity of buildings (especially laboratories) really was. It must also be recognized that these calculations were concerned with short-term economies and were, therefore, inevitably more firmly rooted than some of the others in the particular circumstances applying at Bradford. What the work does demonstrate very clearly is that since capital and maintenance costs are so high (the Bradford figures ranged from 27 to 49% of total costs depending on subject) the potential waste of resources caused by under-utilization of buildings is substantial. This whole question is most worthy of further study particularly as we are now approaching a period when the age structure of university buildings is likely to lead to a significant rise in the need for repairs and maintenance expenditure.

Studies of the Bradford type are technically very demanding, and require great expertise and judgement. It would, for example, make a good deal of difference if senior staff were to be regarded as a fixed cost in the expansion of some particular organization, or alternatively had to be upgraded because of increased responsibilities. While such studies can provide useful insights and illustrate the magnitude of economies that might be available, they do suffer from the drawback of being too detailed and dependent on the situation prevailing in a particular institution to be readily applied at a wider level. To quote a comment on the Bradford work: 'When the UGC tries to calculate the cost of expanding student numbers it cannot examine in detail whether the expansion will entail repeating certain types of teaching meetings in particular universities. What it requires is a marginal cost figure which is some kind of average across departments in different institutions, reflecting the fact that in some of these departments the expansion will simply take up excess capacity in existing classes, while in other departments meetings may have to be repeated.' Attempting to calculate these average marginal costs using the cross-sectional approach formed the basis of a major work on university costs and output by Verry and Davies (1976) from which the quotation above was taken.

The core of this work is a set of cross-section regression analyses relating university costs to various teaching and research outputs. The analysis followed the distinction explained above between departmental costs (for which the analysis concentrated on a few of the most important subject groups) and central costs. Capital costs were excluded. The authors tested a variety of functional forms and output measures but nothing was found to be clearly superior to the simple linear equations:

$$C = \alpha_0 + \alpha_1 U + \alpha_2 P + \alpha_3 r$$

where C represents recurrent departmental costs, U and P represent undergraduate and postgraduate numbers respectively, and r stands for the research hours of academic staff, as derived from a survey organized by the Committee of Vice-Chancellors and Principals (CVCP) on the use of staff time. Similarly for central costs, the favoured equation was of the form:

$$C_c = \beta_0 + \beta_1 \, (\cup_u \text{ ARTS}) + \beta_2 \, (\cup_u \text{ SCIENCE}) + \beta_3 \, (P_u \text{ ARTS})$$
$$+ \beta_4 \, (P_u \text{ SCIENCE}) + \beta_5 \, r$$

where C_c stands for central costs, U, P, and r are as before with the subscript u representing a variable at the university level, while ARTS and SCIENCE denote arts-based and science-based courses respectively.

Given this framework it is the size of the estimated coefficients (the alphas and betas respectively) which determines the cost structure of the system.

There are some serious difficulties with this approach. These include:

a The measures of output, both of teaching and research, are unsatisfactory and, in particular, fail to take account of differences in quality between universities. (Attempts to get at the latter by means of degree classes weighted by earnings differentials were unsuccessful.) This is not necessarily fatal but it does mean that any correlation between university or departmental size and quality will tend to distort the results.

b The observations used for the analysis are not generated by unconstrained decisions by universities and departments: these have to be made within an overall budget which is largely determined by the UGC. This argument is diminished somewhat by the fact that universities are not informed of the precise basis on which the UGC allocates its funds and by the fact that these allocations are not earmarked for particular purposes. It does, nevertheless, have some considerable force.

c The analysis assumes that universities and departments are being observed at an equilibrium point along their respective long-run cost functions. What seems more likely in the circumstances of the time (1968/9) is that universities were at different stages of development with a very variable relationship between capacity, actual student numbers, and unit costs. There is a danger, therefore, that a cross-section analysis will observe, not the long-run cost functions, but a hybrid of long-run and short-run functions.

The authors were well aware of the above (and other) difficulties but felt that, while imposing the need for cautious interpretation, they did not nullify the value of their results. These results related to a wide range of issues but, from our viewpoint, the most interesting were:

a The linear equations imply that marginal costs are constant and that economies of scale depend on the size of the set-up costs.

b The latter were found to be more significant for central costs than at the departmental level.

c The marginal cost of undergraduates was well below the average cost — as little as 40% of the latter in the case of arts subjects.

(This must be qualified: the marginal costs were measured on the assumption that all other outputs remained constant. In other words they did not allow for any concomitant change in research output. The authors did in fact attempt to measure marginal costs which took account of the fact that, in practice, a rise in student numbers would tend to lead to an increase in research: these 'full' marginal costs were much higher but the authors had little confidence in them.)

d   Larger departments seemed to do less research relative to teaching than small ones. Hence the effect of including measures of research in the analysis was to reduce rather than increase the apparent economies of scale.

e   They found no evidence that the volume of research affected the productivity of teaching but did not regard their findings as conclusive on this point.

The main implication of these findings is that there are economies of scale in universities and that these are never exhausted, ie average costs fall indefinitely as student numbers rise. There would, therefore, be no case on cost grounds for ever establishing new departments in existing subjects and even less of an economic case for establishing new universities. The long-run implication would be that the number of universities and departments should be reduced to the minimum possible, hence eliminating unnecessary fixed costs. This line should not, however, be pushed too far. This is partly because the reduction in unit costs attributable to the spreading of the fixed element would eventually become insignificant and easily outweighed by small adverse changes in other factors. More fundamentally it is, as a general rule, very dangerous to extend the interpretation of a regression equation outside the range of observations on which it is based. Indeed, one reason why super-sized departments are not observed may be that, beyond a certain point, diseconomies would set in. This warning applies equally to another of the theoretical implications of constant marginal costs, ie that the allocation of extra students among departments of varying size is a matter of indifference (assuming that the option of closing some is ruled out). The constancy of marginal costs is most unlikely to extend to the case of very small departments.

CONCLUSION
The Bradford and the Verry/Davies approaches are, in some ways, complementary rather than competitive. Both can potentially provide insights and assist in policy formulation but from different angles. The Bradford approach throws light on the details of the peculiar cost relationships to be found in higher education; it provides guidance on the potential for economies of scale and how they can be realized in practice; and, in the latter respect, is of particular usefulness to planners within individual institutions. The Verry/Davies approach is in contrast of little

relevance within individual institutions, the circumstances of which may differ considerably from the average or typical which it seeks to identify. It is designed to serve at the national level to assist with strategic planning decisions, possibly through the incorporation of the results into some kind of macro-model of the system as a whole. Much depends, however, on the weight attached to the problems mentioned above and, consequently, on the confidence which can be placed in the results. Finally, to mention a topic which has not been discussed in this chapter, both methods can potentially inform, though not determine in isolation, decisions relating to the allocation of funds among institutions.

The higher education scene has changed considerably over the last decade, and is likely to change further over the next. Financial constraints are greater than ever, and are likely to intensify as buildings age and student numbers drop. Faced with this challenge, both the approaches discussed in this chapter have something to offer to planners and decision-makers at different levels. As we have noted at various points, however, the work done so far is not immune from criticism and there are many questions still to be answered. That work is also now very dated and rooted in a time when the circumstances and, equally important, the prospective future of higher education were very different. What this adds up to is a pressing need for new work in this area which will tackle some of the problems noted here and help pave the way towards greater cost-effectiveness.

COST-BENEFIT ANALYSIS APPLIED
TO THE CONCEPT OF
ECONOMIES OF SCALE IN HIGHER EDUCATION

Mark Blaug

Are there economies of scale in British higher education, that is, are British universities and polytechnics too small to produce graduates at the lowest possible cost per student? According to the best study we have of the costs of British higher education (Layard and Verry 1975; Verry and Davies 1976), the answer to that question, at least at the undergraduate levels, is an unambiguous 'yes'.

Layard and Verry break down the costs of higher education into teaching and research costs in accordance with the time that members of staff spend on the two activities. Using regression analysis (a statistical technique allowing for the effect of a large number of independent variables, taken one at a time) they calculate the average and marginal recurrent-plus-capital costs of more or fewer students, holding constant the amount of staff time devoted to research. They show that average *teaching* costs for first degrees in universities and polytechnics are invariably higher than marginal costs, the difference being something of the order of 1.5:1 to 2:1. When average costs exceed marginal costs, it follows as a matter of pure arithmetic that additional students will result in a reduction of average costs. In short, there are economies of scale, and indeed considerable economies of scale, in British higher education.

Needless to say, these figures are averages for the whole of British higher education; it is conceivable that they are actually reversed in a few individual institutions. On the basis of a small sample of seven universities and four polytechnics, however, it appears that there are few exceptions to the Layard-Verry generalization (Blaug 1981, pp. 55-65).

If government policy in higher education accorded top priority to minimizing costs per student, it follows that a good many universities and polytechnics should be amalgamated and that closure should be contemplated for, say, five or ten higher education institutions. Obviously, one ought to take account of the transition costs of expanding some institutions and closing others, and it is even possible that these would be so great as to cancel out the long-run savings of fewer, larger institutions. Nevertheless, there would be a general presumption against the present number of higher education institutions in Britain.

Needless to say, present Government policy in higher education is not committed to maximum financial efficiency at whatever cost. Current objectives seem to be to cut public expenditure on higher education as a first order of business. In that case, the evidence about average and marginal costs suggest that the cuts should be concentrated on particular institutions and should not be spread across the board. Be that as it may, there are other aspects of the higher education system that argue for maintaining smaller and not larger universities and polytechnics. The typical British university or polytechnic contains about 3,000 students. By these standards, Oxford and Cambridge, with about 10,000 students, are large. Even these two institutions, however, are not large by American standards: many state universities in America contain 30-35,000 students. A small university or polytechnic may well provide a congenial atmosphere for students and staff. On the other hand, small institutions may restrict the choices open to students in the way of courses and fields of studies. Given the tram-line, specialized first degree of British universities and polytechnics, however, this latter factor counts for little. On grounds of congeniality, therefore, there is a case to be made for small institutions. Oxford and Cambridge with their collegiate system may be said to combine both the financial economies of large size with the atmospheric advantages of small scale. But Oxford and Cambridge, far from reaping the benefits of economies of scale, are actually more expensive per student than most other British universities, in terms, *not of public funds*, but of public plus private funds (Blaug 1980). I doubt, therefore, that they constitute good models of having your cake and eating it too, that is, reaping the cost advantages of being big and also the psychological advantages of being small.

I know of no way of quantifying the educational and psychological advantages of small size, which is to say that I have no way of knowing whether these advantages would be lost if we, say, doubled the size of the typical British institution of higher education. Therefore, I reject the notion that cost-benefit analysis can be simply applied to the question at issue. Cost-benefit analysis consists of a systematic comparison of the quantifiable costs and benefits of an activity, hopefully expressed in monetary terms. We can quantify the costs of higher education and we can even quantify some of its benefits. There is scope, therefore, for the application of cost-benefit analysis to the study of higher education. But many questions of the size of the optimal higher education institution fall outside that scope. What I think we can do is to form a rough judgement about the educational and psychological advantages of small size and then to ask ourselves what we would be prepared to forgo in the way of savings on student costs to reap these particular advantages. It may be that this exercise will yield a crude answer, although I dare say it will yield as many answers as there are individuals making the comparison.

There are those who would resist even this concession to quantification. They say that all the important aspects of size in higher education are non-quantifiable and cannot be compared with quantitative savings in monetary costs. They *say* they cannot be compared but they do in fact compare them because, for them, the quality of life in small institutions outweighs all considerations of greater costs. This may be a satisfying stance to adopt in senior common rooms, but it is, in the first place, illogical and, in the second, impractical, because governments must necessarily make decisions with due attention to public spending on higher education. The burden of proof, therefore, is on the critics of cost-benefit analysis: unless they can somehow place numbers, or brackets around a range of numbers, on the educational value of being small, the case for larger higher education institutions based on cost considerations will sweep all before it.

SOME EFFECTS OF
MERGERS IN FURTHER EDUCATION

Gordon Wheeler

It is an interesting, though sad, commentary on our education system that policies perhaps, and practices certainly, are pursued in a manner subject neither to evaluation nor record. I have been unable to discover any central record of mergers undertaken in the last decade or so, though, no doubt, diligent research could reveal the size of what appears to have been a considerable phenomenon; worse still, no assessment appears to exist of the effects of mergers of colleges of further education (FE) and no knowledge of perceived objectives or results achieved. As might be expected, the random coupling of institutions has on occasion produced some odd offspring, particularly when the genealogies of the parent colleges have themselves included random elements.

CAUSES OF MERGERS

Unlike the mergers which led to the polytechnics, where a single objective was identifiable, or the mergers of colleges of education amongst themselves or with FE colleges, which were based on the need of perpetuating and diversifying, no single cause has led to the merger of colleges of further education. Amongst the causes, or supposed reasons, which it has been possible to identify are the following:

Local Government Reorganization 1974

Colleges merged either because existing multi-campus colleges were spread across two or more of the new authorities or because of the break-up of larger authorities into smaller ones, the new smaller authority choosing to manage its further education on necessarily a new philosophy or pattern, eg in South Wales.

Tertiary College Development

In order to create a tertiary college some existing FE colleges have been merged, often together with school sixth forms to create an institution thought capable of fulfilling changed social or educational objectives, eg in Somerset at Yeovil, Street and Bridgewater.

Conversion of Monotechnic Institutions

Mergers have occurred both amongst a number of mono- (or duo-) technics to create a single college of FE, or on occasion between one monotechnic (eg one art college) and an existing FE college.

Unification
A number of authorities have felt that a more rational, or sometimes fuller, provision of FE services could be provided where a number of small FE colleges could be merged with a hoped for diminution in 'boundary' problems, eg in the Inner London Education Authority (ILEA).

Economy
Changing demands for FE have encouraged mergers which were designed to save on accommodation, staffing and administration. In some instances economies were perceived as deriving from a considerable decrease in the number of senior staff — particularly principals, vice-principals and heads of department, eg in ILEA.

Residualism
Instances have occurred where with the creation of polytechnics or institutions of HE some elements of FE have been left over (or out) — these have been merged to form a new FE college or with an existing FE college, eg at Bristol.

Problem Solving
At least one merger appears to have occurred as a means of removing a 'problem' college from the scene in the hope that its absorption into another college would lead to more effective educational (or financial) control.

This chapter will not deal directly with the creation of the Institutes of Higher Education except to notice that some of the institutions bearing the name are in fact large FE colleges brought about by the merging of small FE colleges with a 'salting' of teacher training.

In passing it might be noticed that there have been few mergers affecting agricultural colleges, and that whilst art colleges have been frequently joined to other educational institutions, music and drama seem to have 'escaped'. A special type of merger has occurred in the establishment of some of the Regional Management Centres, where polytechnics and non polytechnic management departments have seemingly been joined into a 'supra' college organization with a council and a director but no legally separate existence.

The process of merger has been inhibited by several factors:

— the concept of institutional 'life' which has discouraged the formation of new, perhaps temporary, institutions
— the legal differentials between school and FE
— the varying codes of conditions of service and payment covering schools and FE
— the long existing division between the administration of FE and that of schools at national and local level
— *now* the division between institutions and processes under local

authority control and those working under the aegis of other bodies — particularly the Manpower Services Commission.

SOME DISCOVERED EFFECTS

As indicated earlier, no careful monitoring of mergers within FE has occurred to provide some material for this contribution — prepared as it was for discussion in a single group. The opportunity was taken of using the context of the Further Education Staff College to talk to some of those directly affected by mergers. This included both senior staff and teachers, as well as administrators and governors. From the material collected some of the responses make up much of the rest of this paper. The responses quoted are chosen for their interest: no claim is made for their representativeness — they come from those concerned with all areas of public sector FE other than the polytechnics.

Staff

Since most students in FE are within the college for relatively short periods of time (as compared with higher education) it is not surprising that the impact of mergers is most frequently measured by staff and their reactions — and obviously staff react to such changes not only as educationalists assessing relative educational advantages and disadvantages but also as people resisting unwelcome disturbance or enjoying new opportunities and challenges. Amongst negative responses to one particular merger the following is typical:

'Management has become distant and impersonal — delays in decision making have occurred because of the increased college size — the instability of structure before, during and for a time after the merger consumed enormous energy and sapped the will — staff morale has declined as cohesive groups felt threatened and the sheer inconvenience of inter-site travel has either isolated staff from the main stream of activity or, for the staff who have become peripatetic, removed any sense of being on base.'

Another staff member expressed the disadvantages of a series of mergers thus:

'The problem of running a college in these days is in any case large — changing curriculum — students with new needs and the loss of vocational direction are sufficient in themselves to occupy time, energy and enthusiasm. Add to these geographical and social difficulties and the life of teachers becomes untenable.'

Another teacher summarizes thus:

'Geographical: Sites can be quite far apart

Capital resources unevenly spread

Time taken for communications becomes counter-productive

Teachers cannot plan lessons easily if they work on more than one site, since resources have to be spread amongst sites

Social: Conflicts between site/departmental identities

Co-ordination of staff and student groups becomes time-consuming and often ineffective

Central policy decisions reinforce 'conspiracy' theories'

Another comment clearly reflects a personal difficulty:

'I am not comfortable and at ease when I have to go to other sites — I am particularly ill at ease in the staff rooms — I am aware the people from other sites experience similar difficulties. One member of staff spent all coffee and lunch breaks on her own for a long period before she felt sufficiently comfortable in the staff room.'

Many — but not all — mergers result in institutions becoming multi-site institutions and the advantages of the 'larger' institutions are certainly more difficult to enjoy in such circumstances. Many principals and senior staff see as their problem the moulding of site management into an acceptable and effective process of educational management. This is not, however, to suggest that where mergers occur on, or result in, a single site, operational problems disappear — certainly not when the ethos of two merged institutions comes into greatest conflict once it is expressed in a single governing body, academic board or principal. For example, in the joining together of an art college and a technical college the two groups of staff after many years resented their enforced unification and one group attempts to operate outside of the educational and procedural norms of the college of which it has become part. Directives from both the principal and the local authority tend to be ignored and day by day practices in (for example) curriculum planning and presentation do not reflect the wishes of the academic board. The difference in ethos was summed up by one principal who identified staff as perceiving themselves as 'elitists' or 'workers'. This difference seems to be reinforced if the new institution contains elements of FE, perhaps one or two Council for National Academic Awards (CNAA) degrees, whilst the majority of the college work is non-advanced further education and much of that concerned with 'non-academic' courses. Where this occurs a 'fight' develops between non-advanced FE (NAFE) and advanced FE (AFE) and the feeling develops that AFE has the 'upper' hand since not only does AFE support more senior posts but it also becomes involved in seemingly sophisticated processes of validation, certification and external ratification. There are positive reactions as well: a librarian (perhaps used to the multi-site operation of public libraries) reports

'... a staff relatively unperturbed ... when it comes to three academic boards working together, meetings for the most part were amicable and often generated a social warmth rarely (subsequently!) seen.'

Another staff member talks of 'creative tensions deriving from merging colleges having different practices, students, levels of work and types of work have forced colleagues to rethink departmental direction in a more positive way.'

The increased size of colleges has certainly given new opportunities, sometimes eargerly seized: isolated staff members have found colleagues with similar academic interests — in one instance seven economists were able to come together to form a specialist subject group to their mutual personal and professional benefit. In another case general studies teachers found themselves for the first time headed by a dynamic, prestigious individual able to overcome the frustrations which had previously clogged their contribution to college activities. Personal advancement has become easier where in college in-service opportunities derive from merger (eg the marriage of an FE college with a teacher education facility) and for some 'the loss of educational parochialism' has led to a more stimulating and enjoyable life.

Management
It is always possible, indeed quite likely, that the average lecturer is little affected by a merger — the class may still meet in the same place; the syllabus is unaltered but the management is most likely to be changed; one of the economies espoused is that there will be diminution in the number of senior staff — one instance led to the disappearance of three principals, two vice principals, three senior administrative officers and eight heads of department: the personal impact is obvious, the organizational changes are implicit. Greatest difficulty, in these circumstances, can be predicted where some of the deposed office-holders remain on subsidiary levels within a college — but such difficulties disappear with time. Principals of the merged colleges are much concerned with the problems of communication and of role: size tends towards distancing and the role changes as deputies are assigned major function or operational responsibilities (eg resources or staffing), and this together with a more formalized process of internal government calls for skills and qualities little needed in the smaller institutions, whilst at the same time making obsolescent those very capacities which may have been appropriate hitherto.

Since most of the mergers are relatively recent, principals tend to concentrate on two aspects of the college — 'wholeness' and structure. 'The merger has succeeded where staff think of the new colleges as "our college"';

'Some management committed themselves to promoting a "one college" ethos. Staff attitudes to this were mostly apathetic, sometimes hostile' are two typical observations. 'I was forced into a system of issuing college procedures which defined college policy on important topics' — a cri de coeur from a principal who had previously worked on a hypothesis of general consensus.

Some principals see the merger as creative of new managerial possibilities — one was able to adopt a policy of developing specialist services which were quite impracticable before amalgamation — these included three staff concerned with student services, the provision of a part-time medical service, a 'specialist' careers unit and the appointment of three part-time college chaplains.

At head of department level the changed role — implying larger and more significant responsibility — is either welcomed or seen as a burden according to the temperament of the office holder — in this lies an antithesis. The delegation of operation is likely to create stronger departmental units at a time when the 'knitting-together' of discrete units is an underlying reason for the merger.

If mergers continue as they have done, with the decline in the number of colleges the choice of director becomes increasingly significant. Are we moving into a situation where the 160,000 or more staff of FE are going to be managed in perhaps three hundred or even two hundred units instead of the six hundred or more of a decade ago? Are we thinking enough about the management of selection, development, support and tenure? Large comparable institutions in, for example, Canada deny tenure to their senior staff but facilitate frequent sabbaticals! Most of the principals interviewed indicated stress and insufficient support services as their major problems: current public discussion indicates that they are not alone in their concern.

The mergers have demanded experiments in structure and required that questions of purpose and objective be reconsidered. Thus merger is the consequence or the cause (or both) of innovation and of innovation of a more sophisticated kind than that perceived by those who caused the merger to occur. Whilst management is most affected it is noteworthy that unlike industrial comparisons the 'take-over' is rare — the mergers have been caused through actions often remote from the institutions concerned and certainly by public servants or politicians having little knowledge of the institutions or of the probable outcomes.

Educational Results

'Each library benefited by having a wider selection of materials to call upon'.

'The large resources of a big organization can be concentrated for, say, a couple of years in one area and achieve amazing (educational) results.'

'The larger college gave me the opportunity of providing special courses for the unemployed — and for the handicapped. A large college can more readily absorb groups who might, in a smaller college, cause too much concern or disturbance.'

'New groupings of staff led to new courses or better courses — industrial engineers joined design departments: catering infused a biology department with new issues: teacher training was linked to a lively art department.'

'More obviously the welding of traditional sixth form teaching and teachers to the wider curriculum of an FE college with its vocational characteristics has provided stimulus and liveliness — for the sixth form teacher access to adult students has, in particular, facilitated the development of educational method.'

These comments are indicative of the opportunity taken. The disadvantages of diversity, of a loss of specific direction and of the disturbance to reasonable planned growth are equally clear — but less often reported in an educational world where specialization, standardization and simplicity are anathema.

Economic Aspects

Mention has already been made of the specific managerial economy of mergers in FE. The opportunity for rationalization of provision, particularly in urban areas, is real. This opportunity is patently obvious in the provision of full-time 16-19 education — the case for the tertiary college need not be made here. Changing student or industrial demand has frequently led to facilities becoming redundant and this trend must be exacerbated by the current industrial decline. The decrease in the number of firms and of the number of young people in employment is likely to lead to a decrease in specific vocational education related to known industrial and commercial need and its replacement by more general vocational development. Such a process leads to a decrease in the demand for specific vocational facilities (even departments) with the resultant opportunity for provision to be based more upon population trends than upon the specific industrial needs of a locality.

In these circumstances specific vocational resources are likely to be provided but rarely with the result that further mergers in FE will occur.

COMMENT

The range and types of merger in FE have been, and are likely to continue to be, extraordinarily wide. The traditional flexibility of the FE institution — of its leadership and staff — has enabled the processes of merger and redevelopment to be continuous. FE institutions, unlike institutions of higher education, have not been deemed to warrant the manifestations of public outrage when proposals are made for their change, and the absurd hierarchy of education which leaves FE at the lowest level has meant that little public or research attention is given. There seems no good reason why universities or polytechnics should not be as simply merged as are FE colleges and no good reason for 'protecting' institutions providing full-time degree qualifications. Some lessons will not be learned but could well be taught.

a College mergers are only very partially consummated if the resultant institution is characterized by multi-site operation with highly inadequate student and staff transportation.

b The management of integrated (as opposed to federal) institutions requires a highly adaptable and energetic management: that energy may well be present when the merger occurs, but action has to be taken to re-energize.

c The 'external' management of institutions is of special significance: the relationship with the LEA, with HM Inspectorate, with the curriculum bodies, changes significantly as the institution outmatches the specialist skills, knowledge and experience of the external agencies.

d The scale of merged institutions requires new processes of internal management — services provided by national and local authorities are not so much inadequate as inappropriate to an organization dealing with many hundreds of staff and many thousands of clients. Staff and student motivation are largely dependent upon logical and appropriate managerial decisions. The model of educational administration based on schools and universities is unlikely to suffice, particularly so if England ends up with some two hundred major FE (NAFE) institutions. *Either* a changed (more centralized) administration *or* greater delegation is required. An unsteady fence is no place from which to direct complex and precise operations.

The FE experience of mergers is continuous —not having the clearly defined purposes of higher education institutions or of schools the FE institution is, and ought to be, by its nature, flexible, dynamic and adaptive. FE institutions, or more likely some of the staff, will resist some changes, but since fundamental values or processes are not enshrined within the FE institution the lessons to be learned from its experiences are unlikely to be accepted by institutions which, by their nature, are in many ways inhibited from flexibility and adaptability.

APPENDIX: A MERGER CHRONICLED
In one college it was possible to obtain a systematized view of the effects of a complete merger: the comments are those of a principal involved in the merger from his observations and perceptions of what occurred.

PROCESSES	NEGATIVE EFFECTS (Shorter or longer term)	POSITIVE EFFECTS (Shorter or longer term)
INITIAL REACTIONS TO PROPOSAL FOR MERGER	Governors: Rapid waning of interest by some once decision taken – possible poor attendance at Governing Body meetings of constituent colleges LEA officers: Merger seen as opportunity to save resources and to demonstrate economies of scale to elected members who may be 'demanding' savings. Leads to under-resourced new college. Staff: Climate of anxiety engendered.	Governors: Some 'come to life' as political opponents of merger and perceive political advantage. Others perceive opportunities in new and more powerful college – hence need to make good impression and get on to new Governing Body. LEA officers: Opportunity for new working relationship between college and LEA officers in working together over inevitable difficulties caused by a merger. Staff: Opportunities perceived by 'go getters' – involvement in college activities immediately increased.
NEW INSTRUMENT & ARTICLES OF GOVERNMENT. APPOINTMENT OF PRINCIPAL	Uncertainty increases among existing Principals and Vice-Principals which leads to still greater anxiety in general. Tensions increase during merging colleges vying for position of influence – even in a merger! LEA seeks opportunity of increasing its own influence over activities of new college.	Opportunity to set up a better and more influential Governing Body – weeding out mediocre members of previous Governing Bodies.
DEVISING NEW ACADEMIC AND MANAGEMENT STRUCTURES AND PROCEDURES	Confusion and misunderstandings by rank and file staff resulting from historical differences in procedures and perceptions among existing colleges and their continued use.	Opportunity for a new start in devising more appropriate structures for present needs – chance to 'get rid of historic structures and procedures.' Opportunity to change college ethos – very important.
APPOINTMENTS WITHIN NEW DEPARTMENTAL STRUCTURE	Considerable anxiety among senior staff – at ex-Head of Department level – competing for new posts. Resentments among disappointed but senior staff can lead to disruption and ill will. Problems of coping with the possibility of multi-site departments and creating a single department out of several small departments.	Opportunity to weed out ineffective staff at senior level not often available to a college and consequent opportunities to make new and more effective appointments.

PROCESSES	NEGATIVE EFFECTS (Shorter or longer term)	POSITIVE EFFECTS (Shorter or longer term)
COURSE PORTFOLIO	Need for rationalization of duplicated course provision leads to tensions and anxieties. Staff and students may have to move traditional locations.	Possibility of genuine reduction in costs through rationalization of course provision. New and existing courses *may* acquire a better resource base and much stronger political backing with LEA dealing with one large college instead of competing claims of several.
EFFECT ON RANK AND FILE AND STUDENTS	Lack of communication a major problem – rank and file may feel that they no longer know 'management' even as individuals. Loss of direct and immediate contact at Principal and Vice-Principal level. Demand on Student Union leadership much increased – effective leadership may not be available and Student Union activities may be weakened. Rank and file may find increasing difficulty in 'getting through' to new college bureaucracy which seems remote and, probably, less efficient. Ample opportunities for 'cock-ups'	Benefits for rank and file are not immediately obvious but can be present if opportunities for improvement of structures, procedures and ethos seized upon by new management – a slow process as benefits filter down. At the end of the day, for rank and file and students it is hard to convince them that big is beautiful – because it usually isn't!!

DIFFERENCES
BETWEEN THE NOMINAL AND EFFECTIVE SIZES
OF HIGHER EDUCATION INSTITUTIONS

Martin Trow

The issue of potential economies of scale in higher education is a matter of obvious interest to Government agencies which fund higher education, and of potential interest to the colleges and universities which spend those funds. I want to make three points on the issue of scale in higher education.

DEFINING 'SIZE'

First, if we ask what is the size of an educational unit, we must specify what educational or administrative functions we have in mind when asking the question. An illustration from my own situation in California may make this point clear. When someone asks me how large my own university is, one answer is that the University of California at Berkeley has about 29,000 students, perhaps 2,000 regular teaching faculty, and some thousands of other full-time research workers and supporting staff. Those numbers conjure up a picture of a very large academic setting indeed, and so it is, with all of its libraries and laboratories, computer facilities, and student services. But then I must hastily go on to add that as a staff member in that University I hold an appointment in a graduate school with ten full-time regular staff members drawn from various disciplines, and about ninety graduate students, all of us snugly housed in one fake-Tudor building formerly occupied by a fraternity. Most, but not all, of my teaching work is located in that department, as is my academic career, and part, though not all, of my intellectual life. My research work is housed in a quite separate though even smaller research centre. The school (also a department) has its own budget, support staff, Xerox machine, computers, etc. It is one of over a hundred departments and schools on the Berkeley campus. The research centre, free-standing and autonomous, is one of about forty-five at Berkeley.

Berkeley, of course, is one campus of nine that make up the University of California, so another answer to 'how large if your university?' would be: about 120,000 students and 5,500 staff members. Berkeley is in many respects autonomous and self-governing, with its own budget, library, etc. But for some purposes — for example, our relationship with the Government of the State of California which provides the bulk of our operating expenses — the Univeristy is the nine campuses taken together; *that* is the University which is governed by a Board of Regents and which is funded by a block grant from the State.

The point, of course, is that 'the University' is quite different sizes depending on whether one is talking about its finance, its governance, the environments it provides for teaching and learning, the admission of students, or the appointment of staff. And for each of these questions there are many answers, depending on the specific issue and circumstances. For example, to a considerable degree, members of the University can decide on the size of their own teaching or learning environments. Departments vary from eight or nine to eighty or ninety academics; but sub-disciplines within departments can be much smaller, and the effective number of scholarly or scientific colleagues who can read and criticize one's work competently may be very much smaller. The real intellectual community for teachers in a research university is the 'invisible college' of people throughout the world working on the same or closely related problems who read and cite each other's work.

Our students belong to a university of 29,000 or 120,000 depending on whether one is speaking of Berkeley or the University as a whole. But they attend classes that vary from three to 900 students. Moreover, in their third and fourth undergraduate years they are ordinarily 'members' of one of a hundred and twenty-five or so schools and departments of varying size, and their membership depends on the quite varying degrees of intensity of their commitment to their 'major' field. Graduate students, of course, are ordinarily 'members' of departments or professional schools which for them are the locus for the bulk of their studies and formal and informal relations with staff. But students have considerable choice in the size of their classes and in their degree of involvement in their departments. A student with strong academic interests can put himself into a series of close encounters with academic staff members; less highly motivated (or shyer) students, especially undergraduates, can avoid such encounters, and have a profoundly different experience of the University during their nominal membership in it. The University is, in a sense, a holding company for a large number and wide variety of teaching and learning situations. Students who differ in the range and variety of their interests create around them learning environments which differ in size as in other characteristics.

I have been speaking of the context of teaching and learning provided by a university: classes, departments, research units and the like. But much the same could be said of finance or governance in higher education. For some purposes — the shaping of the University budget, or the sum allocated by the State for staff salaries — the unit is the University as a whole; but for the funding of departments the unit is a campus, or a 'college' (a group of departments or professional schools); for the setting of individual salaries, the unit is the staff member's own department, with review by small committees of academics and academic administrators. But this over-simplifies a complex reality: the 'university-wide' administration sets broad policies regarding academic salaries, and these are adapted to the special characteristics of each campus, each department, and each individual staff member by the members of these smaller units.

The governance of the University is a similar but even more complex story, with an enormous variety of different forms of decision-making depending on the issue, and to some extent on the personalities occupying the various positions of authority in the University, campus, department, and academic senate.

Incidentally, the effective 'size' of a department is affected by such things as the importance of academic rank in the governance structure. American universities are relatively egalitarian with respect to most departmental issues, and the size of the governance unit of the department is roughly equal to the number of all of the regular academic staff. In most European universities in the past most academic decisions were taken by the full professors, the 'ordinarie', and this tended to reduce the effective size of the department for many functions and decisions. Ironically, many European institutions were 'reformed' during the late 1960s and early 1970s, and the other members of the academic staff, together with students and non-academic staff, all joined the decision-making process, greatly increasing the effective size of those units for governance purposes. The resulting enormous increase in the complexity of decision-making and the time necessary for discussions and meetings threatened to swamp the academic work of some of those departments. Many of them are still trying to develop governance procedures appropriate to what have suddenly become 'larger' departments for governance and decision-making.

EFFECTIVE SIZE

Second, we can look at the 'effective' size of an academic unit in yet another way, that is, as a reflection of the availability of specific people, ideas, books, or services that a member of the unit may want for teaching and learning. And the 'availability' of these desired sources of knowledge, or the tools for gaining knowledge, is related to the 'opportunity costs' of gaining access to them — 'opportunity costs' being the costs in money or time or energy of actually obtaining those resources. The formal boundaries of academic units have their significance insofar as they define discontinuities in the opportunity costs of gaining access to persons or books or services. In many places, and in much of the past, we have assumed that it is easier to get a book from our own library, or to teach students enrolled in our own institution, or to consult with colleagues in our own department or university, than to do any of those things with the books, students and staff members of other universities. But that is less true as the boundaries of our institutions become more permeable.

We can see this most clearly in regard to the size of a university library. In the past we have thought of a library as a collection of so many books and periodicals — for example, the Berkeley library has over six million volumes. But the opportunity costs of getting a book elsewhere is a different way of defining organizational boundaries or the size of a library, since it defines the actual and not just the nominal availability of the intellectual resources that we are looking for. And those opportunity costs are in turn affected both by the formal and the informal organization of academic units such as a library.

Thus the actual (rather than the nominal) size of an institution can be increased by reducing the opportunity costs of gaining access to intellectual resources across the nominal boundaries of the unit. One illustration: Berkeley's library, as I have said, holds about six million books. But there is another library of almost equal size at Stanford University, about fifty miles south of Berkeley. In principle, its books are available to any scholar or student at Berkeley. But that nominal access is given reality by making a library card to the Berkeley library also honoured at Stanford, and vice versa. And of course, the Stanford card catalogue is available at Berkeley as ours is there. It is no matter that the University of California is a 'public' university and Stanford a 'private' one; in respect to circulation they function almost as one library.

Still, Stanford is fifty miles away. And that could be enough to deter all but the most devoted or specialized scholars from using the Stanford collection. But the two universities have set about to reduce the difference in opportunity costs of using the two libraries to as close to zero as possible. They have, among other things, instituted a free bus service between the two universities (the Gutenberg Express, as it is called) that runs three times a day and that carries people and books between Berkeley and Stanford. If I call my library and ask for a book, the library service will not bother to tell me whether the book is in Berkeley or in Stanford; they simply accept a commitment to get the book for me. And when it is delivered to my office, I may see for the first time whether it comes from Berkeley or from Stanford, or has been borrowed from yet another library on the West Coast. Most of the time I pay no attention to whose library it comes from.

Of course, the Gutenberg Express will also carry me down to Stanford if I want to go and browse in the library there, or use a reserve collection, or indeed, if I just want to see a friend or colleague over lunch. The Express is a free service for movement of books or people between the two universities; it is available both to staff and students, and it is a service that makes it relatively easy, among other things, for Berkeley students to take courses at Stanford or to consult their staff or to use their library, at least within the time constraints of the bus schedule.

As we can see, the Gutenberg Express, by reducing the opportunity costs of gaining access to Stanford, has changed the operative size of Berkeley, as it has of Stanford, at least for teaching and learning, though not for finance and governance, where the formal boundaries of institutions are more consequential.

There are of course devoted scholars at both institutions who need to go through documents which perhaps only exist at the other, and they would travel up and back no matter what the difficulties; indeed they might travel 6,000 miles if they had to. But there are many more casual scholars who would not bother to get a missing book if it meant a substantial delay. The system I have described is devoted not only to reducing opportunity costs to teachers and staff, but to reducing them so far as possible to zero.

The great problem under those conditions is information overload. It becomes so easy to get books (or other kinds of information) that one is continually being inundated with information, creating a different set of problems arising around how to manage one's time in the face of relatively easy access to so many people, books and ideas.

An analogy is the functional use of the long-distance telephone as a research instrument by mathematicians. The new generation of young mathematicians, unlike their elders, will simply pick up the telephone and call Geneva or Tokyo to chat with friends or colleagues about research problems they are currently working on. And the use of the telephone in that way simply modifies the effective size of their institutions — it brings the 'invisible college' directly into their studies, creating something like a continuous scholarly conference.

Obviously there are very different answers to the question 'How large is your library?' The answer really depends on the opportunity costs, and the availability of books under different circumstances. A similar story could be told if one asks a student how many courses of study are available to him. The number begins to approach infinity, since in California he can choose from all the courses that are offered at Berkeley at any given time; he can choose from all the courses offered on any other campus in the University for credit at Berkeley; he can, with some slight further bureaucratic arrangements, choose from all the courses offered at Stanford for credit at Berkeley, and he can also take courses in the colleges of the State university system. In other words, the whole machinery of higher education is designed to make more and more courses available to him. He has to have extremely esoteric tastes indeed not to find what he wants very close to home. But nevertheless, the principle of the transferable credit and the elective system affects the operative size of Berkeley as a context for teaching and learning in respect to taking courses at Stanford or on other campuses of the University — although the opportunity costs of taking courses elsewhere is rather higher than in getting books from the libraries of those institutions. But nevertheless, the effect is to reduce those costs and to encourage the use of facilities on other campuses and in other universities.

I have said that the links between Berkeley and Stanford greatly increase the size of both libraries, that is to say, the operative size of the library to the user, for relatively little money — the cost of operating the Gutenberg Express and the associated book retrieval services. But the question might be asked: should the libraries be linked only for circulation, or should they not also be linked for acquisitions and planning? That introduces a rather different dimension of cost savings linked to scale. Berkeley and Stanford are beginning to coordinate acquisitions. But I think there is a certain reluctance on the part of any big university to voluntarily surrender its comprehensive library, its ability to offer on its own campus a very wide range of books and periodicals. And that, needless to say, is increasingly expensive. I am surprised that public authorities, both in California and in

Britain, still support the tremendous expense required to give academics the very large local libraries that they continue to demand, though I think increasingly as part of a status claim, part of the historical definition of a great university. How long the public authorities will be prepared to do that is uncertain, though the state authorities are also bemused by the historically close connection between the status and prestige of a university and the size of its library.

But we are in perhaps some danger of collapsing the great libraries into a myriad of electronic signals. If books become available in some way on computers, and if whole books or pieces of them can be printed out quickly, what would it mean then for a university to have a central library of its own? And the question will then arise: what are the opportunity costs of organizing a university that way, even as those costs change very rapidly? Real and difficult new questions will arise, having to do with such issues as how an electronic library will affect browsing, what it will do to undergraduate teaching, etc. Moreover, computer-based libraries will surely be used very differently by chemists and historians, by senior scholars and first-year students. The needs and patterns of library use of these groups differ greatly, as do the effects of any reform of library services, including the changes in their boundaries (and thus their effective size) resulting from new technologies of information storage, retrieval and transfer. The blurring of institutional boundaries for educational purposes may cause problems for financial and administrative managers, for whom nominal legal boundaries have a reality in budgets and employment contracts. This strain perhaps accounts for the very high opportunity costs still levied by many institutions on their members who want to cross boundaries. But the problems are not insurmountable, though the attitudes around them are stubborn and difficult to change.

ADAPTABILITY OF BUDGETS
Third, I have so far been speaking to the issue of the scale of academic units as this is related to the availability of people, ideas and other intellectual resources, stressing that academic units can be both much smaller than their nominal size, when looked at as collections of intellectual environments for teaching and learning, and also much larger, if their boundaries are made less relevant by reducing the opportunity costs of crossing them.

A third perspective on the scale of academic units touches on their ability to deploy resources quickly. And here I believe we see distinct advantages in large nominal size. For the ability to respond quickly to new needs in a university — for example, the ability to provide seed money for a good research idea, to provide staff and resources to a new field of study, to arrange a scientific conference quickly or invite visiting scholars — all depend on the existence of what economists call 'slack', institutional resources of money, space, time or energy, that are not already committed to some existing function or ongoing activity. I think there is a close connection between the existence of substantial 'slack' resources and the creative intellectual life of a college or university. It is these resources, uncommitted but available, and the freedom to assign them quickly to spontaneous interests and activities, that encourage and reward creativity and enthusiasm among staff and students. For those purposes, putting resources at the service of exciting ideas quickly, institutional 'slack' is absolutely crucial. One of the great costs — perhaps the greatest cost — of severe budget cuts in higher education, and of the bureaucratization and rationalization of teaching and learning more generally, is that ordinarily 'slack' goes first. And that has large, though mostly invisible, detrimental effects on the intellectual life of a college or university; it is difficult to assess the cost to science, scholarship or society of things that do *not* happen.

But whatever the state of the budget, large units have an advantage over small ones because, on the whole, the bigger the budgetary unit, the more nooks and crannies there are for hiding 'slack' resources, and the more fat there is for the support of initiatives and innovations.

Of course, this is not always the case. For example, in the United States the rationalization of primary and secondary school operations has been carried very far, and there is relatively little slack in those institutions (which I suspect partly acounts for why the intellectual life in them is not as lively as it might be). But fortunately, our institutions of higher education are not yet so well managed; the diversity of what we do, and the esoteric nature of so much of it, protect us to some degree from the effects of severe rationalization — except in times of severe budget cuts. That in turn may account for why rationalizers are on the whole hostile to diversity in higher education and dubious about the claims of academics to arcane or esoteric knowledge.

The defence of 'slack' in higher education in the face of legitimate calls for economy and pressing alternative uses for those resources is hard at all times, and especially difficult in times of declining resources. But it is almost impossible to defend uncommitted resources in the face of modern methods of financial management and accountability in higher education. 'Slack' is a function of loose fiscal management, a diversity of funding sources, the survival of organizational anomalies, and above all, of relations of trust between funding agencies and the institutions of higher education. All of these supports for slack are under pressure, but other things being equal, large institutions can still find those extra resources — so essential to teaching and learning, though so indefensible to government agencies.

One practical recommendation that arises out of this discussion is to increase the operative size of our colleges and universities by reducing the opportunity costs of crossing their boundaries; and then finding some way of retaining the savings that flow from the resulting economies of scale for the functions and activities that are dependent on slack or uncommitted funds. We in higher education need to be as creative in the defence of our resources as are others in their expropriation of them. A clearer understanding of the difference between the nominal and the effective size of our institutions may be helpful here. The boundaries for funding of colleges and universities are pretty rigid, and often defined by public law or administrative practice. The boundaries of our institutions as places for teaching and learning are not so constrained; they are, as we have seen, more flexible and permeable. We must find some way to exploit that important difference in the way we view the 'size' of our institutions when we look at them legally and financially, or as centres for teaching and learning.

INSTITUTIONAL SIZE, HIGHER EDUCATION AND STUDENT DEVELOPMENT

Russell Thomas and Arthur Chickering

Major social changes have raised issues concerning institutional size in Europe and the United States during the past twenty years. The first change is the 'massification' of higher education which occurred as a result of the 'baby boom' during World War II, and the pressures for increased access to education at all levels. This change first caused rapid expansion of enrolments at the elementary and secondary levels, which in turn led to rapid expansion of demand for higher education during the 1960s (Bereday 1973). The second change, felt increasingly during the decade of the 1970s, is the increasing cost of education combined with growing economic pressures resulting from both inflation and economic decline. The consequence has been both uncontrolled growth of most existing institutions and efforts to realize the apparent savings resulting from consolidation and increased size. This consolidation has been evidenced by growing numbers of mergers in the world of business and industry, and by creating consolidated or regional schools and large scale, comprehensive universities. But juxtaposed to these dominant trends has been the development of small businesses, industries and educational institutions. Many of these have emerged as single purpose, sharply focused institutions with clearly defined missions and priorities. These different approaches have been based on contrasting philosophies and assumptions concerning relationships among purposes, size, and consequences for desired outcomes. These variations have also provided a basis for research which has examined relationships among differences in size, ongoing experiences and apparent results. This paper examines some of those philosophies and the evidence concerning psycho-social development, which seem to be related to variations in size.

CONTRASTING PHILOSOPHIES

Perhaps Schumacher (1973) puts the issues best when he says: 'In the affairs of men there always appears to be a need for at least two things simultaneously, which, on the face of it, seem to be incompatible and to exclude one another. We always need both freedom and order. We need the freedom of lots and lots of small, autonomous units, and, at the same time, the orderliness of large scale, possibly global, unity and coordination' (1973, p.65).

'What I wish to emphasize is the duality of the human requirements when it comes to the question of size: there is no single answer. For his different purposes man needs many different structures, both small ones and large ones, some exclusive and some comprehensive. ... Today we suffer an almost universal idolatry of giantism. It is therefore necessary to insist on the virtues of smallness — where this applies.'

'The question of scale might be put in another way: what is needed in all these matters is to discriminate, to get things sorted out. For every activity there is a certain appropriate scale, and the more active and intimate the activity, the smaller the number of people that can take part, the greater is the number of such relationship arrangements that need to be established. ... What scale is appropriate? It depends on what we are trying to do' (1973, pp.65-66).

Sale (1980) asserts that in higher education, as in a number of other areas, 'human scale' is appropriate whether we are referring to business, government or education. 'Human scale' is 'a scale at which one can feel a degree of control over the processes of life, at which individuals become neighbours and lovers instead of just acquaintances and ciphers, makers and creators instead of just users and consumers, participants and protagonists instead of just voters and taxpayers' (1980, p.39).

Implicit in these two orientations is the concern that Western culture has created structures which ignore human needs and characteristics. Several obvious developments which occurred in colleges and universities in the wake of the burgeoning enrolments of the 60s support the views expressed above. Many institutions created ombudsmen and other support services designed to counter the escalating depersonalization and bureaucratization. Student protest, using the IBM card as a symbol, decried this depersonalization. The buildings constructed then with their high rise dormitories, libraries and classrooms stand as brick and mortar testimony to the attempts to realize savings in construction and in administration judged to result from substantial increases in unit size. The human problems which seem to be inherent in such structures are catalogued by Sale (1980), who notes that 'it is true that the bigger the skyscrapers become, the more costly, less efficient, less adaptive, less safe and usually the more hideous they are.' And Sale's observations are supported by the high crime rates and vandalism associated with high rise urban development apartments as well with similar college and university structures.

MYTHS AND REALITIES CONCERNING INSTITUTIONAL SIZE

Sale (1980) cites five major myths and provides evidence concerning the contrasting realities:

1   'Larger units are more economical.' In fact there seems to be a curvilinear relationship between size, costs, and productivity. 'There seem to be no clear connections between the economies of scale of a particular plant and the success of that company' (1980, p.311).

2   'Larger units are more efficient.' In fact, large scale corporations or large scale institutions are less efficient in energy use, in use of raw materials, and notably, in the use of human resources. They also generate more waste. And 'wastage' in higher education is

greatest at the largest public institutions. Indeed a number of studies have indicated detrimental consequences resulting from increased unit size.

3 'Larger units are more innovative.' In fact, most significant inventions during the 20th Century have come from individual inventors operating completely on their own or autonomously within institutions. Most educational innovations have occurred in small colleges rather than large universities.

4 'Larger units provide goods and services at a cheaper price.' In fact, costs of production, advertising, promotion and packaging result in higher prices.

5 'Larger units are more profitable.' In fact, findings repeatedly demonstrate that as corporate size increases profit rates decrease or remain constant.

DEFINITION OF APPROPRIATE SIZE

One of the most useful conceptual frameworks and some of the most powerful data concerning relationships between size, human experience, and developmental consequences come from the work of Roger Barker and his associates. Their studies of differences associated with school size are particularly pertinent. Barker (1964) begins by looking at the interaction among three variables: numbers of 'settings', varieties of settings, and numbers of persons per setting. A 'setting' has two major components: behaviour, and the objects with which behaviour is transacted. The behaviour and objects within a setting are organized in non-random fashion and the boundaries of a setting are usually quite clear. The persons who inhabit a setting are often interchangeable while the setting remains fairly constant. A living room, for example, is a behaviour setting. It differs in expected behaviours and objects from a kitchen or a bedroom. Living room behaviour across families is more similar than living room and kitchen behaviour within the same family. Similarly classrooms, campuses, factories, production lines, playgrounds, are all settings. Table 6.1 presents findings concerning variations in settings, varieties and persons for schools of differing size. The table shows that as schools increase in size the number of persons increases much faster than the number of settings or varieties of settings. In the smallest school there were about 2 *settings* for each person; in the largest school these were more than four *persons* for each setting.

What are some of the consequences of those differences in school size for the experiences and learning of the students? Here are some of the key findings:

Students in small schools held an average of 3.5 responsible positions per student (members of play casts, officers or organizations, members of musical groups, members of athletic teams); students in large schools averaged .5 responsible positions per student. Put differently, on the average, in the large schools every other student held a single position; in the

Table 6.1[a]   SIZE, SETTING, AND STUDENTS

School	Community Population	School Enrolment	Settings	Students per Setting	Varieties of Settings
Otan	199	35	60	0.58	29
Dorset	169	45	58	0.78	28
Walker	450	83	96	0.86	31
Malden	507	92	78	1.18	33
Meadow[b]	–	113	94	1.20	32
Midwest	781	117	107	1.09	33
Vernon	1,150	151	98	1.54	29
Haven	2,907	221	154	1.44	36
Eakins[c]	551	339	139	2.44	34
Booth	3,004	438	218	2.01	39
University City	23,296	945	312	3.03	36
Shereton[c]	4,739	1,923	487	3.95	41
Capital City	101,155	2,287	499	4.58	43

[a] Adapted from Tables 4.1 and 4.3, pp. 42 and 49, Barker and Gump 1964.
[b] Meadow was two miles from the nearest town; it served two towns.
[c] High school that served several communities in addition to the one in which it was located.

small, each student held two positions. Furthermore, students in small schools held twice as many different kinds of responsible positions as those in large.

Students in small schools received twice as many pressures to participate, or to meet the expectations of the school, as those in large; and academically marginal students in small schools received almost five times the pressures to participate as those in large.

Self-evaluations of students in small schools were based on the adequacy of their contributions and on their level of competence in relation to the job requirements; self-evaluations of students in large schools were based on comparison with others.

Students in large schools exceeded those in the small in satisfying experiences related to vicarious enjoyment of others' activities.

Students in small schools exceeded those in large schools in satisfying experiences related to the development of competence, to being challenged, and to engaging in important activities.

Students in small schools tended to achieve relatively limited development in a wide variety of areas while those in large tended to achieve greater development in more narrow or specialized areas.

Barker uses the term 'redundant' to describe the condition where the ratio of persons to settings becomes unfavourable. Redundancy, therefore, is five persons for a game of bridge, three persons to carry a suitcase, ten persons for an octet, twenty persons on a trout stream, 2,000 persons on a small strip of beach. It's when the best man joins the honeymooners. It's a class of eighty with a 'class play' that calls for twelve. In general redundancy occurs when the number of inhabitants of a setting leads to decreasing opportunities for satisfaction and participation for each individual.

There seem to be six general consequences associated with increasing redundancy.

a A smaller proportion of the 'inhabitants' actively participate.

b The activities and responsibilities of those who do participate become less varied and more specialized.

c Persons with marginal ability are left out, ignored, and actively denied opportunities to participate.

d Evaluation of performance shifts from how well a person's abilities actually fit the requirements for participation, for a given position, or for an area of responsibility, to how good one person is compared to another; in educational terms, evaluation shifts from criterion referenced evaluation to norm referenced evaluation. Furthermore, as numbers increase and put pressures on the need to discriminate, judgements are made on the basis of increasingly fine distinctions.

e A hierarchy of prestige and power develops.

f Rules for conduct, definitions of appropriate behaviours, standards for performance, become increasingly formalized and rigid.

These findings are consistent with the research synthesized by Sale and with the thinking of E.F. Schumacher mentioned above. They are consistent with results found by those who have studied the effects of size in factories, public agencies, discussion groups, and other task groups.

The dynamics which underlie these results are quite straightforward. It is not surprising, therefore, that they are consistent across a wide range of settings. Behaviour settings offer a variety of satisfactions and opportunities that individuals find attractive. When the number of persons is low there are more opportunities to participate per person; thus each experiences the attractions with greater force. In task-oriented settings, there are functions to be carried out that impose obligations on the participants. When manpower is low, each participant has to assume more responsibilities and each becomes the focus for more obligations. Under such conditions individuals perceive more clearly the importance of their own participation and that of others. Thus, feelings of loyalty or responsibility are added to the initial intrinsic satisfactions that attracted the individuals in the first place.

In addition to these internal or personal forces, if the setting has importance as part of a larger context, external pressures will increase as manpower diminishes. There will be more invitations or demands and the social rewards for contribution will increase. At the same time requirements for admission or for certain kinds of positions will become more liberal. Thus persons who usually might only be spectators will be pressed into service; reticent followers more often will find themselves in leadership roles. In this way, those who under circumstances of overpopulation might be seen as unsuitable or marginal, under conditions of limited manpower or underpopulation find themselves in demand.

The appropriate size of an institution, then, is determined by examining the numbers and variety of settings, the range of activities and responsibilities required, and the numbers of persons needed to carry out those activities and responsibilities effectively. In short, the appropriate size is that which avoids making individuals redundant. If the institution's purposes are educational, or if the organization providing goods and services is also concerned about creating a developmentally challenging environment, then the ratio of persons to settings and the associated activities should be such that each person experiences (a) a reasonable level of demand and (b) sufficient variety of challenges. Furthermore, the ratio should be such that their contributions are apparent to themselves and others, and such that there are frequent opportunities to develop new areas of competence and understanding.

SIZE, INSTITUTIONAL CHARACTERISTICS AND STUDENT EXPERIENCES

With the conceptual perspectives and research findings of Barker, Sale, and Schumacher as background, we are ready to look more directly at empirical studies of relationships between size differences, institutional characteristics and student experiences. We report results in four major areas: institutional ethos and sense of community; student participation; faculty concern for students; and persistence and retention.

Institutional Ethos and Sense of Community

Douglas Heath (1981), based on twenty years of research concerning relationships between college characteristics and student development, documents the significance of a clearly defined institutional ethos as discernible character, identity, climate. Smaller institutions find it easier to establish and maintain a clear-cut identity which, in turn, communicates more clearly to students what the institution stands for, the values it holds, the outcomes it desires for its graduates. Students selecting such an institution are more likely to achieve a good fit between their objectives and those of the college, to find their motivation reinforced, and to enter more actively the educational opportunities provided. These dynamics have been documented in a number of studies. Eddy (1959), reporting his study of college influence on student character said, 'The potential of the environment is measurably increased by a feeling of community. And that feeling appears to begin where it should — in common understanding and acceptance of commonly shared goals' (pp.143-144). Jacob's (1957) survey of research concerning the effects of college on attitudes and values found little influence except at a few institutions where a distinctive climate prevailed.

Figure 6.1 INSTITUTIONAL OBJECTIVES EXPRESSED AS MOST AND LEAST DESIRED CHARACTERISTICS OF GRADUATES

FOUR MOST DESIRED	FOUR LEAST DESIRED
Savior	
Educated in the liberal arts within the context of a Christian world view	Independent member of society
	Recognizes and accepts feelings as relevant to decisions
Committed to Christ	Chooses friends carefully
Guided by God's will	Educated in the traditional liberal arts
Activated by Christian ideals in the various pursuits of life	
Elder	
Capable of effective judgment based on sound analysis of relevant information	Chooses friends carefully
	Committed to Christ
	Guided by God's will
Activated by the intellectual, cultural, moral, and spiritual values of our civilization	Mixes easily but chooses friends carefully
Constructive and creative member of interdependent society	
Socially responsible and a participating citizen	
Kildew	
Has understanding of self as an individual and as a member of society	Committed to Christ
	Guided by God's will
	Dedicated to Christian service
Constructive and creative member of interdependent society	Educated in the liberal arts within the context of a Christian world view
Capable of effective judgment based on sound analysis of relevant information	
Able to recognize and develop own creative potentials	

Chickering, A.W. 'The Best Colleges Have the Least Effect' *Saturday Review* January 16, 1971

There can be sharp differences in institutional ethos and associated values. Figure 6.1 comes from Chickering's longitudinal study of student development in small colleges. The most and least desired characteristics for graduates are in direct contrast. The important thing about these data is not whether one agrees or disagrees with the particular characteristics desired; the important thing is the clarity of purpose and institutional character, and the consequent developmental power of these small institutions (Chickering 1971). That's why research by Chickering, Astin, and others finds that many podunk colleges — small, poor, little known institutions — often turn out to foster more substantial student development than larger, comprehensive, well supported institutions with elaborate facilities, strong research productivity, and high powered faculty members.

In these days of rapid change and economic stringency, such institutions also have a good prognosis for survival. On the basis of his research, Heath (1981) hypothesizes that those colleges that will adapt healthily and effectively to the demands of the future are more accurately and reflectively aware of themselves, empathically responsive, internally coherent, stably resilient and autonomously distinctive (p. 93). So a clear institutional ethos not only has solid consequences for student development, it has survival value as well. These qualities are much more readily achieved in small institutions than in large complex units with all their problems of internal communication, organizational coherence, cumbersome decision-making processes, and multiple agendas (Gallant and Prothero 1972). Such institutions send mixed messages to students as well as mixed messages to faculty and staff.

In institutions with underpopulated settings, all participants will know one another more fully, will have more and more diverse opportunities to work and play together, more challenges to develop healthy cooperative relationships. In large overpopulated settings, the proportion of the community known and the level of information about fellow community members become much more limited (Wallace 1966). Depersonalization escalates. Students create subcultures which insulate them from more general identification with the institution, its purposes, and its values.

Participation
Alexander Astin (1977), drawing on his multi-institutional research, reports that 'the small, frequently single sexed, selective private college was found to have the most widespread effects, primarily because of the involvement and opportunity for participation available.' This finding is consistent with Barker's findings that underpopulated settings require everyone's involvement in order for the work of the setting to be accomplished. Overspecialization, which characterizes overpopulated settings, encourages only the most competent to actively participate (Gallant and Prothero 1972).

Faculty Concern for Students

Bayer (1975) found that 'size was the attribute most highly correlated with the criterion: the larger the institution, the less was the concern for the individual student (p. 557).' Pascarella (1980) noted that 'present evidence suggests that institutional size is negatively associated with amount of student-faculty non-classroom contact' (p. 563). Numerous studies have found that the quality and frequency of student-faculty contact is a key variable in student development. Admiration of faculty is associated with higher grade point averages and also affects graduate school aspirations. Faculty encouragement is a major influence in going on to graduate school (Davis 1964.) Thistlethwaite (1960) on the basis of his multi-college research, describes the faculty member who stimulates graduate study:

'He does not see students only during office hours or by appointment; open displays of emotion are not likely to embarrass him; students need not wait to be called upon before speaking in class; in talking with students he frequently refers to his colleagues by their first names; students don't feel obligated to address him as "professor" or "doctor"' (p. 189).

Now, of course, there are many faculty members who share these characteristics in large, comprehensive institutions. The problem is that the institutional ethos does not usually support substantial interaction with students, and they are hard to find among their less interested colleagues. Most importantly, as Astin's work (1963) has made clear, faculty attention is usually reserved only for the best and the brightest. Those average or marginal students who would be most helped by the friendship, support, and encouragement of key faculty members seldom have the courage to seek them out and are seldom recognized by the professors themselves.

Persistence and Retention

Numerous studies demonstrate that persistence and retention is highest where students have a keen sense of involvement, have frequent informal contacts with the faculty, and experience a caring attitude on the part of the institution and its staff. A comprehensive report concerning retention by Beal and Noel (1980) identified 'inadequate student faculty contact, lack of faculty care and concern, and inadequate academic advising' as three of the top five negative campus characteristics in relation to retention. Conversely, they found that the top positive characteristics were 'caring attitude of faculty and staff, high quality of advising, and student involvement in campus.' Obviously, it is difficult to have much influence on students if they do not stay with us long enough to experience what we have to offer in any significant way. Thus the fundamental consequences concerning retention are basic to all the other variables concerning institutional characteristics and student experiences.

INSTITUTIONAL SIZE AND DEVELOPMENT OUTCOMES

The general evidence concerning relationships between institutional characteristics, student experiences, and developmental outcomes is by now substantial and clear. Major studies have been reported by Astin (1977), Brawer (1973), Chickering (1969), Katz (1968), Newcomb et al. (1967), Raushenbush (1964), Solomon and Taubman (1973), Winter, McClelland and Stewart (1981); major syntheses of the literature have been presented by Feldman and Newcomb (1970), and by Bowen (1977). These studies demonstrate that the institutional characteristics and student experiences mentioned above are key variables which influence student development. Because institutional size is related to such variables, it is not surprising that size also appears as a variable in more direct studies of developmental outcomes. But, unfortunately, empirical studies which examine direct relationships between size and developmental outcomes are still scarce. We report results for three major areas: achievement, competence, and sense of competence; attitudes and values; satisfaction.These findings are remarkably consistent with those discovered by Barker and his associates in their studies of school size, and the underlying dynamics seem to apply as well.

Achievement, Competence, and Sense of Competence

Astin's multi-institutional research (1977) shows a clear advantage for small institutions in this area. Compared to those at large institutions, those at small colleges are more involved in academic studies, in honours programs, and athletic activities. They interact more with the faculty concerning their academic studies. They evidence greater achievement in leadership skills, journalism, and athletic ability. Smith and Bernstein (1979) note that many small residential institutions, by virtue of their curricular coherence and shared educational experiences, foster communication among students concerning intellectual issues. And it is through just such informal discussions and debates that critical thinking skills are sharply honed. Chickering (1969) suggests that institutional size has special consequences for achieving a strong sense of competence. When evaluation shifts from a focus on how one's competence matches up against particular tasks or responsibilities (criterion referenced evaluation) to how good one is in relation to a large number of peers (norm referenced evaluation), then by definition, a high proportion of the students come out 'average' or below. Sense of competence flourishes when there are opportunities to cope with a wide range of challenging problems, to test oneself in varied situations, to work with a diverse range of persons on significant tasks. As such opportunities become more constrained and as competition for those increasingly scarce opportunities becomes tougher and tougher, then a strong sense of competence is hard to sustain. Astin's research concerning differential college effects on the motivation of talented students to obtain the PhD (1963) documents these dynamics. Institutional size was the second most important variable which had a negative effect on PhD aspirations. (The first variable was percentage of males.)

Values and Attitudes
Changes in attitudes and values associated with differences in institutional size tend to be more qualitative than quantitative. Astin (1977) reports that differences in size seem to be related to differences in effects. Small institutions seem to foster a greater degree of altruism and intellectual self-esteem (sense of competence again); large institutions encourage increased liberalism, hedonism and 'religious apostasy'. The most striking difference was between the altruism found among students at small institutions and the increased hedonism found at large institutions. Note that these findings are highly congruent with the Barker findings concerning the effects of under-populated settings on sense of responsibility and on the importance of individual contributions to community activities and needs (Barker and Gump 1964).

Satisfaction
The differences in satisfaction also tend to be qualitative rather than quantitative. Students in small institutions express greater satisfaction in their relationships with faculty and with the quality of classroom teaching; those at large institutions express greater satisfaction with the variety of courses, the quality of the science program, and the emphasis on social life. These data are also consistent with the Barker findings concerning specialization, and the development of more narrow areas of competence in large schools versus the more broad-gauged development which occurred for students in small schools.

SOME HYPOTHESES FOR FURTHER RESEARCH*
Although direct studies of relationships between institutional size and development outcomes for college and university students is still scarce, there is enough theory and research to justify some clear hypotheses which might be the basis for further study. Before venturing our hypotheses, however, we want to make clear several basic dynamics which encourage human development. According to Erik Erikson (1950) and Nevitt Sanford (1966), there are three conditions which maximize the possibility for significant learning and personal development. They are: first, the opportunity to engage in varied experiences and to assume diverse roles and responsibilities; second, meaningful achievement in areas important both to the person and to others whose judgement and opinions are valued; and, third, relative freedom from anxiety and pressure, so that the risks associated with tackling new tasks, assuming challenging responsibilities, and trying out new roles and relationships are reasonable; so that the consequences of venturing into

---

*cf. Chickering (1969)

those new arenas are not likely to be devastating to self-esteem or to one's future plans and aspirations.

Few colleges and universities meet these conditions. Norm referenced grading systems, and detailed curricular requirements, combined with shoddy and highly subjective methods and criteria for evaluation work, directly counter the self-testing in diverse situations which fosters significant learning. High academic pressure under competitive conditions makes thinking for oneself risky and rewards conformity to conventional wisdom and prescribed expectations; exposing areas of weakness and testing areas of limited competence can jeopardize academic success and future possibilities. Meaningful work and active contribution to real problems can counterbalance narrow role definitions and limited repertoires. But most college work is academic. It seldom asks students to tackle real-life situations where performance can make a difference. Smith (1966) found these forces strongly at work with Peace Corps volunteers. He reports, 'important personality changes in the direction of maturity were frequent. I think I know why. ... Once in, most of them saw and were captured by the challenges of the job and role: students and schools needed everything they could give, a window on Africa that invited exploration. Their effective motivation was emergent: a response to opportunities and difficulties as challenges to be met, not as frustrations to be endured or "adjusted to". ... It was the high degree of committed but disinterested investment in a challenging undertaking, I think, that was so auspicious for psychological change in the direction of maturity. Experiences from which the self is held in reserve do not change the self; profit in growth requires investment' (pp. 565, 566). Few institutions of higher education provide such opportunities as part of their academic programs.

A second major principle is that learning and personal development occur through recurrent cycles of differentiation and integration (Sanford 1962). *Differentiation* and *integration* refer to a familiar process. Development occurs as persons encounter new conditions and experiences for which they must develop new courage, competence, and attitudes. The process is analogous to Dewey's (1938) 'reconstruction of experience', Festinger's (1957) 'cognitive dissonance', Heider's (1958) 'balance theory', Newcomb's (1943) 'strain for symmetry', Helson's (1964) adaptation level theory, and Rogers's (1961) development of congruence. Differentiation and integration, challenge and response, then are basic processes to keep in mind when considering interactions between institutional characteristics, student experiences and developmental change. Expressions of discomfort, signs of upset are not necessarily negative indicators. On the contrary they may be evidence that developmentally fruitful encounters are occurring, that stimuli for learning and development are being experienced.

A third major principle is that individual differences influence the outcomes of particular experiences. The impact of a given curriculum, course, teacher, book, or field experience will vary according to the characteristics of the student who experiences it. Helson (1966) says:

'We must distinguish between the *physical* stimulus and the *effective* stimulus. ... The effective stimulus depends upon the state of the organism, upon the preceding and accompanying stimuli, and, in some cases, upon possible future outcomes of stimulation ... most of the difficulties of stimulus theories of motivation vanish if we take as the zero of intensity not the absolute threshold (the level at which a stimulus can barely be perceived) but the adaptation level. It then follows that stimuli below level as well as above level may possess motivating power because it is discrepancy from level in either direction that determines affective quality and its distinctiveness' (pp. 144, 147).

So it is for college students. The stimulus value, the motivational force, of a curriculum, course, institutional ethos, relationship with a faculty member, significant reading or discussion, an internship or field experience, will vary depending upon what the student has been used to and what his or her purposes are. Zero stimulation occurs when college turns out to be no different from secondary school or, conversely, when the challenges are so great given the student's prior background that effective response is impossible.

With these basic principles in mind let's turn to our hypotheses concerning institutional size and human development. We use our definition of appropriate size and Barker's concept of redundancy as our size variable. We propose relationships between redundancy and the development of intellectual competence, sense of competence, identity, and integrity.

Intellectual Competence
Under conditions of redundancy, less development of intellectual competence will occur. Because of fewer opportunities to deal with problems of significance, and because fewer challenges are encountered, intellectual skills and working knowledge will be less fully developed. Some students who are particularly talented, or strongly motivated, or who catch the interest of a faculty member, or who capture a position on the college paper or debating team, for example, may develop to a high degree in a particular area. But for most students, development will be less than it would be if they were not so redundant.

Sense of Competence
Under conditions of redundancy sense of competence will be less fully developed. Because of fewer opportunities to hold positions of leadership and responsibility, and because of fewer opportunities for active mastery and successful coping with a wide range of tasks, sense of competence will develop less fully, will rest on a more limited basis, and will operate in a more limited sphere. The shift in the basis of self-evaluation may have even

more significance for sense of competence than the limited opportunities for significant achievement. As self-evaluation comes to be based primarily upon comparisons with others, it is difficult to see oneself as very competent. Those who are better in the areas to which one aspires are highly visible; there seem to be so many of them up there in front. Those less skilled are quite invisible and their presence carries little force. Because by definition only a few can be on top, the rest struggle along, frequently using as much energy to cope with feelings of inadequacy as to cope with the tasks at hand. But when the emphasis is on who can do the job and who is willing to undertake it, and where esteem and respect derive from the successful completion of significant tasks rather than from relative standing, there is a more accessible and solid basis for learning where competencies lie and how far they extend.

Development of Identity
Under conditions of redundancy development of identity will be more limited. If opportunities for active participation and involvement are limited, and if the variety of environments and activities is limited, then so are the opportunities for the kinds of self-discovery, or 'resonance testing', through which a full and rich sense of identity may come about. If only rarely can one get behind a wheel — and if then one can drive only on a country lane, in sunshine, with an automatic transmission — then not much development occurs and one feels uncomfortable if other conditions must be faced. Of course, a similar result occurs if one drives only through snow and mud with smooth tires in a car without a heater.

The response to the combination of limited opportunities and competitive pressure is often observed. In secondary schools there is the too frequent settling on either beauty, brains, or athletic prowess as the centre of one's self-esteem, as the core of one's being. In college it takes more particular forms: the 'beats', the 'grinds', the 'party boys', and others. However, when opportunities are many and varied and when competitive pressures are lessened, one can range more widely, can relax one's grip on those roles found satisfying. The increased range of vicarious experiences available to the person in the overpopulated setting may somewhat compensate for the decreased opportunities for more active participation, but they do not provide the experience of self-testing on which a sense of identity ultimately is built.

Development of Integrity
Under conditions of redundancy development of integrity will be more limited. The development of integrity involves two steps. The first step requires clarification of the values to which one is committed and which provide the major organizers for one's words and deeds. The second step involves achieving congruence and internal consistency between word and word, word and deed, deed and deed. Clarification of values occurs when

one must make choices which influence the lives of others and where the effects of those choices are observable. The context may be a committee to consider parietal rules, or a dormitory meeting to deal with a problem of noise or stealing, or an honour system. Value choices reside wherever decisions must be made regarding the living conditions in the college community; in underpopulated settings the opportunity for each individual to confront problems and to think through alternatives occurs more frequently. Similarly, where there are few individuals, the impact on the whole of the behaviour of each is significant and observable. A student working with a group of five or ten others, or living in a house of twenty or thirty, sees quickly and clearly the consequences of his choices for the lives of others.

Limited size carries particular force for the development of congruence. When the totality of a student's behaviour is visible to many others with whom he goes to class and to parties, sits on committees and in general meetings, it is difficult to talk one kind of life and to live another. Thus the development of congruence is significantly related to institutional size and organization.

IN CONCLUSION

There are other aspects of student development for which institutional size has implications, but those described are probably the ones most affected. The basic point is that as redundancy occurs, less development is fostered. Redundancy occurs when increases in the number of inhabitants lead to decreasing opportunities for participation and satisfaction for each individual, when manpower exceeds what is needed for the jobs to be done.

As redundancy sets in, the activities and responsibilities of those who do participate become more specialized and those with marginal qualifications are more quickly and more completely left out. A hierarchy of prestige and power develops and evaluation shifts from an emphasis on the fit between abilities and the requirements of a job, to an emphasis on how one person compares with another. Rules and standards for conduct become more formalized and rigid.

Under such conditions, the opportunities to cope with significant problems become more limited and challenges to existing skills and knowledge are encountered less frequently. Experience becomes less varied and self-testing more restricted. The range of different persons to be dealt with in contexts important to one's own life decreases, and situations provoking examination of values and consideration of the consequences of one's actions less often have to be faced. Thus, development of competence is more limited except when supported by special ability or special motivation. The development of identity, and the development of a personal value system are fostered less under conditions of redundancy than they are when the ratio of students to settings is smaller.

Some institutions with very large enrolments are developing creative ways of increasing the number of settings and reducing the number of persons in each. Many colleges with small enrolments have not capitalized on their condition and are rapidly increasing enrolments without concurrent increases in the number and variety of settings available to students. The basic point is that an institution should be large enough so that each student frequently must confront and operate within a variety of significant settings, but not so large that he becomes superfluous and disappears in the lonely crowd.

THE PROBLEM OF SCALE IN HIGHER EDUCATION

Christian Schumacher

SOME SALIENT ISSUES

In British industry, there is a continuing debate on the virtues or otherwise of the 'economies of scale'. Fifteen years ago, for example, the then Chairman of the British Steel Corporation, Sir Monty Finniston, epitomized the 'Big is Best' philosophy when he launched the massive investments of the early 1970s. A symbol of his faith in large scale was the gigantic blastfurnace at Redcar — the largest in Europe — capable of producing 10,000 tonnes of iron per day. In the boardroom at Redcar there used to be a photograph of the blastfurnace with an outline of St. Paul's cathedral superimposed upon it, drawn to scale. The blastfurnace was bigger than St Paul's.

Fifteen years on, the tide is turning. At the Royal Society of Arts a few months ago, the present Chairman of the British Steel Corporation, Mr. Ian McGregor, chaired a Cantor lecture given by one of his senior managers entitled 'Innovation in the Steel Industry, the Vice of Scale'. Now, too, many new investments, both in steel and elsewhere, are on a smaller scale than before for sound commercial and social reasons. Very large corporations are decentralizing into quasi-autonomous units of a more manageable size. There has been a revival of interest in the small business.

Industry's interest in the economies and diseconomies of scale is understandable, since scale is a prime determinant of cost and hence of profit. The units to be measured are tangible, material resources such as machinery, plant and buildings and energy; and in the case of manufacturing, construction, mining, distribution and several service industries, a visible product with a money value. The effects of scale on the production of a good or a service can be fairly easily ascertained.

In higher education, however, the issues surrounding the economies of scale are much more nebulous. Firstly, the 'products' of universities and other institutions of higher learning are not objects which can be transacted through the medium of money. The student has to be 'prepared for life'; the researcher is occupied in the 'pursuit of knowledge'. How is one to relate the effects of scale to such objectives? Secondly, on what basis should scale itself be measured? The number of students per teacher? The size of department? The number of departments administratively united under a common management? The size of university building? The area of the campus in square metres? The number of books in a library, or the number of libraries in a university? Indeed, should the university be the unit of measurement, or the college or the library?

WHAT IS SCALE?

The word 'scale' belongs to the category of relations, in that its meaning is defined by a comparison between two things. A college with 300 students is small in scale in relation to a college with 500 students and large in relation to a college with 100 students.

The notion of an economy or diseconomy of scale involves a second order comparison. It relates *changes* in size to *changes* in the ratio of input to output. Thus if a college of 500 students is cheaper to run per student than a college of 300 students there is an economy of scale. However, in this example the output measurement, ie the raw number of students, is purely quantitative and ignores any qualitative measure of output, eg the students' educational attainment or their subjective experience of living in a college of a given size.

A simple measure such as the raw number of students has, however, advantages over more sophisticated indices. It is objective and unambiguous and avoids subjective value judgements about quality. Also the number of students relates in a real way to the quantity of resources and effort needed, in that whatever the level of his educational attainment may be, every student has to be fed and housed and the physical facilities provided for his education and recreation.

To begin with, therefore, we shall take the number of students as a simple indicator of output.

LEVELS OF ANALYSIS

Within the educational system as a whole, several levels of analysis may be distinguished, any of which may be used as a measure of scale from the point of view of *input*. Seven main levels are described as follows.

The Primary Component

The most basic units of input are the individual material products which are used each day or week in the running of a university or other educational establishment: food for the kitchens; utensils; cleaning materials; stationery, books; office equipment; teaching aids from chalk to audio-visual appliances; scientific instruments and laboratory equipment; tools and loose supplies; fuel; maintenance items; and so on.

Staff

Although the staff are also a basic input, they are not on the same level as primary components in the sense that people are not just another input like energy or materials. The primary components have to be manipulated by staff to be used effectively.

The Unit of Work

When primary components are manipulated by staff, the result is the third level of analysis: a unit of work. We are talking here about the interface between the teacher, his teaching aids and his students (or, for that matter, between the chef, the kitchen utensils and the food). This level is the basic building block of all institutions, whether educational or industrial. The manner in which this interface is handled will determine the extent to which the 'raw materials' (whether food or student) are actually *transformed*. In the case of a student, for example, the unit of work will be an element in his transformation towards the acquisition of greater knowledge.

The Department

A single unit of work on its own, however, does not fully realize the total teaching objective. The transfer of the required degree of knowledge or competence is usually obtained as a result of cumulative learning and practice and from the interaction of several teachers. A student has to participate in a large number of units of work on his journey towards maturity, just as when a meal is prepared or administration is carried out a succession of different activities has to be undertaken. As far as the formal structure of the university is concerned, the cluster or network of units of work through which the student must pass is usually the responsibility of the *Department* or *Faculty*. In a well organized department these units will be carefully linked to each other, so that while each is devoted to a small part of the total transformation process, they are nevertheless each an integrated part of a well-rounded syllabus.

The College

In order to obtain effective synchronization between departments and to link the 'learning' with the 'living' dimension of the university, a structure larger than the department has to be created and sustained. In some universities this is the level of the college. The college is greater than the sum of its departments in two ways. First, it is a physical asset which provides a location both for the formal educational and informal social life of its members. Second, it is an administrative centre which directs, plans and controls the running of day-to-day activities. Thus the college provides the organizational framework within which the work of the various departments can proceed smoothly. In addition to the departments directly devoted to the attainment of the main educational objectives, a college will contain several supporting or ancillary functions such as accounts, catering, maintenance, and so on.

The University

Put together a number of colleges and the next level of analysis is created: the university. A university may comprise several colleges in different locations or it may be synonymous with a single college. It is, however, more than the sum of the colleges, since it possesses powers and rights not possessed by the colleges themselves. For example, it sets examinations; it awards degrees; it receives grants and finance; it represents its constitutent colleges in the outside world; it provides common facilities for use by its members; it possesses certain regulatory powers; it is responsible for safeguarding the future of its constituent colleges; and so on. The university, in short, performs a number of *corporate* functions not carried out by the colleges or departments themselves.

The Higher Education System
Finally, individual universities collectively form part of the higher education system. No learning institution is an 'island unto itself' and all universities are dependant upon a myriad of organizations which not only provide specialist services but influence the parameters within which each separate institution can operate. For example, the University Grants Committee's role is to oversee the allocation of finance; that of the CNAA to ensure fair and universal standards of examination; that of UCCA to facilitate student admissions, and so on. Behind these lie the regulatory powers of the Government's Department of Education and Science.

SOME ECONOMIES OF SCALE IN HIGHER EDUCATION
If one compares input costs per student for different unit sizes, it can be shown that at each level economies of scale are to be found. Let us briefly summarize what these are.

Primary Component Economies
Primary component economies can occur when materials or operating supplies are purchased in bulk, since big buyers can exert more purchasing power than smaller ones and obtain price discounts. Also, some reductions in unit costs (per student) are possible through bulk handling in certain cases.

Staff Economies
Staff economies may exist when large numbers of people are deployed within a single organization, since the larger the number of people the easier it is to allocate work so as to obtain minimum manning. Also, there may be savings in administrative functions arising through the principle of division of labour.

Unit of Work Economies
Unit of work economies arise when the proportion of primary components and staff allocated to students falls. In its simplest form large classes are cheaper to run than small ones.

Departmental Economies
Departmental economies arise mainly because as size rises it is often possible to pool the resources of the department more effectively and so reduce unit costs, ie to rationalize teaching (and administration) by balancing peaks and troughs in workload. Also there are the so-called economies of 'massed

resources' which allow a department undertaking a large number of identical functions to carry a smaller contingency budget, because it can assume for statistical reasons that not all its resources will malfunction at the same time.

College Economies

College economies also exist, notably through the ability of larger colleges to spread their fixed costs more widely. Both a small and a large college, for example, will probably need only one or two caretakers, gardeners or porters at the front lodge. Also a large college can usually afford to invest proportionately more in capital-intensive facilities (eg computerized accounts) with consequent economies thereafter. Again large buildings are in general proportionately cheaper to build and maintain than smaller ones. This follows from the mathematical axiom that the larger the size of a three-dimensional structure the less its surface area rises (representing capital costs) in relation to its volume (representing usage).

University Economies

In the university, costs per student may fall as size rises in so far as a larger university can better utilize specialist resources to underpin its activities, eg careers office, investment management. Indirect cost savings may be obtained through better expertise resulting from specialization; also the size of these functions seldom rises in proportion to the mainstream activities of the university.

Education System Economies

Finally, education system economies can increase with scale because in larger systems there is a greater opportunity for more efficient resource allocation, and also because the larger the market for educational consumables the greater the economies from mass production in the industries supplying goods and services to the educational system.

DISECONOMIES OF SCALE

While each level within the educational system offers quantifiable economies of scale, there are also many diseconomies to be found. We are not referring here to the diseconomies which an increase of unit to an absurd size will entail in the sense of the well-known adage that a giant ten times the weight of a human being will collapse under his own weight. We are referring to the fact that under certain conditions *the economies of scale achieved at one level can create side-effects which directly generate diseconomies at other levels.* For example, the economies of scale achieved at the level of the primary component may lead to diseconomies at the level of the department, college or university. Or oversized colleges may create diseconomies at the level of staff or unit of work, and so on. Let us take as a specific example the diseconomies which arise from an excessive size of college.

First, a very large college creates a diseconomy at the level of the primary component through a *decrease in the quality of managerial control*. This arises because communication lines are longer between purchaser and client and so there is a greater likelihood of inappropriate and wasteful buying practices. For example, one department may specify a requirement peculiar to itself which is then inappropriately imposed on all other departments. Also, in larger organizations there tend to be greater status feuds between departments with each demanding as much as, if not more than, every other department.

A very large college also creates diseconomies at the level of staff because it becomes progressively difficult, as size rises, for staff to identity with their college. Their identification is with their own sub-group whose interest can easily conflict with those of the college as a whole. There is a *narrowing down of the work contract*, in that staff can busy themselves in their own affairs without regard for the interests or reputation of the college, even though (as in times of financial crisis for example) its needs may be critical.

The unit of work can also suffer if embedded in a very large college. This is partly because where there is a large bureaucratic administration the *capacity to change and improve diminishes*. Complexity leads to inflexibility: it is more difficult to obtain new books (eg from a very large library) or materials; classes are confined to specific rooms, often without adequate facilities; support from the college infrastructure is less readily available, or only exists in a standardized, depersonalized form; and so on.

Similarly, bureaucratic inefficiencies create diseconomies at the level of the department when the college is too large. The greater difficulty in scheduling rooms, lecture theatres, etc, necessitates *greater administrative effort*. Senior department staff spend a greater proportion of their time in college and non-departmental affairs. The college is less able to boost a successful department or push up the standards in an unsuccessful one. Perhaps above all, in a very large college the supporting or functional departments tend to become ends in themselves and, despite their own large size, frequently are unable to provide a cost-effective level of support.

Finally, within a multi-college university or indeed within the educational system as a whole, very large colleges can acquire a disproportionate influence in decisions relating to the *allocation of resources*, which as a result may be misallocated. A good example is the allocation of students to colleges when the total university intake is shrinking. It is undesirable to allow a large college to run at below full capacity since it is less able to recover its total costs than a smaller college. It therefore becomes a priority to give preference to the large colleges even though the smaller ones may be more cost-effective and attain higher educational standards. Analogous processes apply for social and political reasons in the more extreme cases when closure of specific colleges is contemplated.

One could go on and describe in detail the diseconomies of scale which rub off from the economies found at each of the other levels. Space does not permit, however, and so the main relationships have been summarized in table 7.1. The table is, of course, schematic and the designations will not be applicable in all cases. Their purpose is simply to emphasize that the issues surrounding the economies of scale debate in education (as indeed in industry) should not be conducted from the partial perspective of any single level, nor from the point of view of any single likely effect. The issues are systematic and global and should be treated as such.

SOME CONCEPTUAL DIFFICULTIES

The analysis may now be used to explain why students of scale in higher education are almost universally agreed that while there are economies of scale to be realized from having bigger universities or colleges, they nevertheless feel uncomfortable with the strict conclusion that each country should invest in a few giant establishments. This discomfort arises for two main reasons. First, a change in university size carries with it diseconomies not only at the lower levels within itself, but also at the higher level of the educational system as a whole. That is to say, although a large-scale college or university itself may appear to spend less money per student than a smaller one, in so doing it creates diseconomies which have to be borne by the educational community as a whole. These costs are, however, only borne indirectly and collectively by individual establishments, because they express themselves through the general inefficiency of the educational system as a whole, a lack of overall resources, apparently excessive and arbitrary interference by the State and so on. It might be demonstrable for example that the cost per student in a large university was, say, £3,000 compared with £3,500 in a smaller one. Nonetheless, what remains unproven is whether within an educational system in which the overall balance between economies and diseconomies was the most favourable there would not be, in the long term, average costs of, say, £2,500 per student.

It is worth mentioning that a similar situation exists in industry where firms bear the accumulated costs of excessive scale through the collective burden they place on the infrastructure, as well as through an industry-wide lack of competitiveness compared with imports, a consequent national balance of payments problem, inflation and high interest charges, and so on. But, since they bear the costs collectively, they are, or appear to be, unaffected by them *in relation to one another* and therefore continue to plan and invest on a nationally excessive scale.

A second reason why economies of scale in higher education are not singlemindedly pursued is that people acknowledge that a crude quantitative measure of the number of students inadequately reflects the true objectives of a system of higher education. These are qualitative as well as quantitative and they are often subjective and complex, and sometimes conflicting.

For the purposes of this paper four main qualitative objectives may be distinguished:

— *teaching,* for the transfer of knowledge and 'the ability to think'
— *research,* for the pursuit of new knowledge

Table 7.1 SUMMARY: ECONOMIES AND DISECONOMIES OF SCALE

Large scale / Effects on:	Primary Components	Staff	Unit of Work	Department	College	University	Educational System
Primary Components	BULK PURCHASING	Repetitive work, fatigue	Under-utilization. Over-standardization	Redundancy	Overstocking	Vulnerability to suppliers	Waste
Staff	Higher consumption rates	SPECIALIZATION OF STAFF	Duplication	Demarcation	Overmanning	Militant trade unions	Excessive staff costs
Unit of work	Provisioning problems	Alienation	TECHNICAL ECONOMIES OF SCALE	Timetable	Lack of facilities	Poor reputation	Poor value for money
Department	Supply/demand bottlenecks	Poor communications, low productivity	Irregular supervision	POOLED RESOURCES	'Tail wags dog'	Unmanageability, disinterest of course context	Over-centralization of expertise
College	Poor control	Isolation. Poor motivation. Higher absenteeism	Improvement delays	Administrative inflexibility	LOWER FIXED COSTS	Lack of power at centre	Misallocation of reserves
University	Supply shortages	Remoteness from society	Irrelevance	Separation	Inadequate support	SPECIALIST SERVICES	Geographical over-concentration
Educational system	Supply breakdowns	Powerlessness. Politicization	Tendency to reductionism	Lack of relevance to society	Misdirected investment	Intellectual vulnerability	WIDER EDUCATIONAL OPPORTUNITIES

Key Capitals: ECONOMIES OF SCALE Lower case: Diseconomies of scale

— *resource,* for the dissemination of knowledge to the wider community
— *moral,*   for the social and psychological development of the student
       as a person.

THE PRIMARY LEVEL

It should by now be apparent that as far as the economies of scale are
concerned there is no simple answer to the question: how big should a
university be? Nor are conventional methods of research, in which the
quantifiable changes in a chosen variable are measured against a set of
controlled factors, likely to yield satisfactory results. The task is rather to
find the best balance of costs throughout all levels so that the total cost for
the system as a whole is as low as possible. The solution should also be
compatible with the four main educational objectives mentioned.

One way of going about such an endeavour is to start with the notion of
the *primary level*. This is the level which most directly embodies the main
objectives of the total system. It gives the answer to the question *why* the
other levels exist. In the case of the *teaching objective* the primary level is the
level at which the teaching actually takes place, ie the department or faculty.
The other levels exist to support the process which goes on at the primary
level. Their raison d'être is to provide the materials, staff, facilities and
buildings, legal and financial assistance, and so on, which are needed to
facilitate the primary task. Conceivably, the teaching function could be
carried out, albeit primitively, without the assistance of the other levels. The
other levels, by contrast, have no justification without the teaching
departments.

The other objectives also have their own primary levels. In the case of
research it is also the department, although this does not have to be
synonymous with the teaching department. As a *resource* for the wider
community, the primary level is the university itself; while in its relation to
the *moral* objective, it could be argued that the primary level is to be found in
the college, where most social encounter takes place.

OPTIMUM SCALE AT THE PRIMARY LEVEL

Since the primary level embodies the purpose of the organization, it is
obviously vital that this level is structured in such a way that the purpose can
be achieved most effectively. Scale is one variable in this structuring process.
Economies of scale are only justifiable in so far as they do not seriously
inhibit the attainment of the main objectives. What, then, are the crucial
variables which determine whether a department performs well or not?

There are, of course, a large number and everyone will have his own ideas
as to which are the most important. The ones we are most concerned with
here are *structural* as opposed to *procedural* or *personal* variables. Thus,
we will not directly consider the adequacy of the personal relationship
between the teacher and student, the demographic composition of the

university population, the qualifications and experience of the teaching staff; nor the procedures governing entry, discipline, termination or other aspects of the treatment of students during their course, important though they may be. What we are concerned with here are the physical and organizational boundaries within which the teaching process is carried out. These include the determination of the limits of the subject discipline to be taught within the department; the size of the department in terms of the numbers of teachers and students; its physical size and layout; its internal organization; its responsibilities for organizing its own work and for ensuring that proper standards are met; and the department's dependence upon, or independence from, other departments. Each of these variables will affect the degree to which the department will successfully achieve its teaching objectives. Similar considerations apply to the attainment of the other objectives such as research.

As far as scale is concerned the most important variables are: the limits to the intellectual discipline; the number of teachers and students in the department; and the physical size of the facilities dedicated to its work. In so far as different combinations of these will determine the resulting scale, they may be termed *prime determinants* of scale. They are also the variables which link the issue of scale to the main objective, since the structure of each of them impacts significantly on the quality of teaching that takes place. Therefore it is necessary to determine the best way of structuring the three variables in order to obtain the highest quality of teaching. When this is done the optimum scale of a department may be deduced.

Limits of the Discipline

Theoretically, there are an indefinite number of ways to divide knowledge into disciplines. During the past century universities conventionally distinguished between the arts and the sciences. More recently, it has been convenient to divide between the physical sciences (eg physics, biology, chemistry, engineering); the social sciences (eg psychology, sociology, economics, human geography, history, social anthropology); the moral sciences (eg law, medicine, education; and the liberal arts (eg languages, art, music).

It is beyond the scope of this chapter to discuss whether these 'broad brush' divisions are appropriate or whether individual disciplines within them are still valid in contemporary society. In the context of the debate on scale we will assume that they are reasonably apposite.

The range and combination of disciplines taught in individual universities and other higher education institutions varies widely, from large universities offering a comprehensive range of subjects to specialized vocational colleges which teach one particular discipline (eg medicine, education, furniture-making) to a considerable depth. The formal object of teaching is, however, the same in all these cases, at least at undergraduate level. It is that at the end of the course the student must have attained and be evaluated in a certain level of knowledge and ability in a certain range of subjects, which together cover the syllabus.

Where the syllabus is general and covers a wide span of knowledge the level of understanding in any particular aspect is likely to be relatively superficial. Where the syllabus is focused and vocational the degree of knowledge expected at the end of the learning period will be much deeper. Thus in a *multi-disciplinary* syllabus, eg PPE, the student will be expected to acquire a relatively shallow degree of knowledge in the *single disciplines* contained within it. In a syllabus covering a single discipline, a deeper knowledge will be required of its several constituent *subject areas*, eg the subject area of statistics in the discipline of economics. If the syllabus only covers a single subject area, a considerable degree of knowledge will be expected to the level of the various *topics* contained within the subject, and so on. Whatever the degree of specialization of the syllabus, in other words, the student will be expected to attain appropriate academic standards corresponding to the level immediately below it; and will be examined in several papers covering the subject matter at this level (with possibly one or two special subjects at the level below).

In addition to the student's learning task we also need to consider the level of knowledge and experience which the *teacher* should possess to be able to teach his subject satisfactorily. It goes without saying that he needs a qualitatively finer and more mature knowledge than the student. Quantitatively, too, his grasp should probably extend well into the level *below* that which is required of the student in his examinations.

The Structural Conditions for Optimum Teaching

Obviously, there are many conditions for good teaching; above all, perhaps, personal and procedural ones. Here, however, structure is our concern, and it raises the basic question: what is the optimum number of teachers needed to cover *with excellence* the subject matter contained in a typical university syllabus?

It is highly unlikely that any *single teacher* will be able to achieve sufficient expertise in all the subjects covered in the syllabus since the arena of knowledge is almost limitless. Even a single subject within the syllabus (such as that corresponding to an examination paper) should, if possible, be taught by more than one teacher, on several grounds:

— additional teachers can provide cover for absence
— the subject area is more comprehensively covered by the combined knowledge of several minds
— one student will relate better to one teacher, a second to another
— several teachers employed in the same subject can interchange experience to their mutual advantage
— variety in teaching stimulates student motivation.

On the other hand, there is obviously also an *upper limit* to the number of teachers able to share meaningfully in the planning, organizing, teaching and examining of a particular subject. When numbers grow too large, fresh and frank exchange of views becomes inhibited, mutual sharing falls, the intimacy of the small group is lost, time is lacking for full and creative participation, communications splinter, the cohesion of the group weakens, the dominant clique can distort the curriculum, innovation is stifled.

Above all, effective learning by the student is inhibited. Exposed to fragmented teaching, he loses the sense of 'wholeness' essential for learning. Observing the lack of mutuality among those from whom he seeks wisdom, he easily becomes alienated. The raison d'être of the university — to teach well — is overlooked.

What, then, is the 'right' number of teachers who together can provide the optimum quality and quantity of resource for maximum learning? From a purely structural point of view, the research evidence from students of small group dynamics suggests that *best results are achieved by the primary group, of say, 2 - 5 persons* (Hare 1962). In this size of group, friendship and participation are maximized, creativity and decision-making are at their peak, communication lines are very short, and the level of informality and understanding are most conducive to the attainment of high motivation.

In short, there is a good case for arguing that teaching should be organized so that a *core group* of up to five or so teachers is responsible for each of the main areas of knowledge covered in the syllabus. As already explained, this knowledge area will correspond broadly to the level below that of the syllabus as a whole. This level may be termed the *core subject* level, and may be regarded as synonymous (for practical purposes) with the subject matter covered in one of the 6 - 8 main examination papers covering the syllabus as a whole. When a 'core group' collaborates in the teaching of a 'core subject', there is a correspondence or 'match' between the technical interrelationships which exist between the different aspects of the subject matter and the social and intellectual relationships present within the small group. The two reinforce each other.

The 'Ideal' Size of Department

A 'match' between the 'core group' and the 'core subject' is the cornerstone from which we can now construct the ideal size of department. Such a construction will inevitably be somewhat arbitrary, as all structural generalizations are. The method of approach is to ensure that a department contains enough teachers to cover adequately the teaching of the syllabus, yet not too many so as to make administration and the personal care of the teaching staff unmanageable.

The number of teachers needed to cover the syllabus will depend on the number of 'core subjects' it contains and the extent of overlap by teachers into other 'core subject' areas. On the empirically observable assumption that a typical syllabus will contain 6 - 8 'core subjects' and that each teacher will be a member of an average of two 'core groups', it is easy to calculate that an average-sized teaching department should not consist of more than 12 - 20 teaching staff.

This size of department supports very well research findings in industry which have shown that it is difficult to ensure effective management and administrative control, as well as high productivity, group cohesion and motivation, when the number of persons in a first-line organizational unit exceeds about 15 - 20 people (Miller and Rice 1967; Work Research Unit 1978). Just as the primary group of 2 - 5 appears to be best for a creative interchange, so the secondary group of 12 — 20 is optimum for the purposes of control.

To obtain the 'ideal' size of department in terms of the number of students, one need simply apply an agreed *student/teacher ratio* to the above figures. Here, there appears to be a consensus that the ratio in a university should be considerably lower than that typically found in secondary education, where 1 teacher to 30 pupils is not uncommon. Ideally, it could be argued that the ratio for creative learning at a university should be in the same range as the primary group for the same reasons as were given above. On the other hand, the cold wind of financial reality has led to an empirical ratio in the UK which is somewhat higher, on average about 10:1. Applying this latter ratio gives a maximum department size of 200 students, or three overlapping sets of 66 per year in a three-year course.

The Research Objective

As far as *research* is concerned, the primary level of analysis is also the department, as has been mentioned. The question arises, however, as to whether the *same* department should undertake research as well as teaching; and, if so, whether the same 'core group' should be materially involved in both.

A useful insight into this issue may be obtained from industry where an analogous problem is to decide whether different *businesses* can be run effectively using the same human resources. There, it has become abundantly clear that it is almost always counter-productive to pursue different objectives using the same personnel. Industrialists have learnt that different businesses demand different selling techniques; dissimilar production strategies, development priorities and time-spans for decision-making; and varying mixtures of skills and experience.

It is probable that similar considerations apply to higher education in the case for separating teaching from research, certainly at the level of the individual teacher or researcher:

— The best teachers usually possess quite different temperaments and skills to the best researchers.

- At undergraduate level the teacher needs a wide breadth of knowledge, the researcher a deeper if relatively narrower understanding of his subject.
- Currently university teachers are too often evaluated on their research output, to their disadvantage.
- Students taught by researchers can be taught too much detail about too narrow a subject area, so their syllabus is fragmented.
- Conflicts can arise between teaching and research priorities.
- Researchers seldom spend enough time preparing for teaching and seldom seek improvements to their teaching methodology.

There is, in short, a case for suggesting that as a general rule 'core groups' of teachers should not be required to undertake long-term serious research, and vice versa for researchers. The objectives are different, the subject areas are different, time spans are different and the skills required are different. Different people should therefore be involved and different criteria for selection, performance evaluation and setting of work priorities should apply.

On the other hand, there is clearly also a close connection between teaching and research when they relate to the *same core subject*, certainly from the point of view of their intellectual complementarity if not the need for administrative co-ordination. It therefore makes sense that the two should be linked together, not at the creative level of the primary group, but at the organizational level of the secondary group, ie at the level of the department. A small group of researchers should thus augment the teaching staff in each department — providing, of course, that the total size of department is still within the limits of good management.

THE COLLEGE AND THE UNIVERSITY

Space does not unfortunately permit a full discussion of the 'moral' and 'resource' objectives of higher education to be found at the levels of the college and university respectively. In both cases, however, it is possible to argue with some weight that the objectives cannot be successfully met in very large scale institutions.

As far as the size of college is concerned, the main structural condition for meeting the 'moral' objective is the achievement of suffcient *internal differentiation* of working facilities, social areas and residential quarters so that a real sense of community and fellowship may be built up, while at the same time preserving a sense of propriety between the sexes. Whether it is possible to safeguard these human needs within a single gigantic physical structure, or whether several free-standing buildings are necessary remains an open question. Experience in the hotel industry suggests that there is an upper limit in building size beyond which it becomes much more difficult to cater for the individual requirements of the guests, despite the sub-division of the hotel organization into floor, and sometimes corridor-based departments. Moreover, the financially most successful hotels seem to be those in the medium size range, ie 50 - 100 bedrooms. As a rule of thumb, therefore, one might envisage within a university, colleges of a similar size range, with each being appropriately internally differentiated.

Although we have so far made the assumption that the college contains a number of (smaller) academic departments, and in addition performs residential, social and administrative functions, this formation is not essential. In many higher education establishments, the departmental or faculty structure is vested in the level of the university and not the college. In both cases, however, the same methodology as has been used in relation to department size may be applied to decide on the most appropriate scale at the higher levels. Thus one would not expect to find maximum efficiency, or cost-effectiveness, in a college containing more than about twenty administrative and teaching departments; nor in a university containing more than twenty colleges and/or twenty faculties.

Finally, given the fact that the maximum sized faculty should contain not more than 200 students, we come to the conclusion that the maximum size of university compatible with the attainment of its major objectives should be about 4,000 students. It should be stressed, however, that this is an upper limit figure. If one takes the lower end of the range into account, *an optimum sized university should contain between twelve and twenty departments and thus a total of between about 1,500 and 4,000 students.* Medium-sized universities within this range have the additional advantage that, because there would have to be more of them, they could be evenly dispersed geographically, thus providing a necessary cultural and intellectual resource throughout the country.

FINANCIAL IMPLICATIONS

We have attempted to show that a university of between 1,500 and 4,000 people has, from a structural standpoint, a better opportunity to achieve its main objectives than larger universities. It now remains to demonstrate that this size range also offers the maximum *overall* economies of scale, as well as maximum qualitative advantages. That is to say, we need to show that the net sum of all the economies and diseconomies of scale is the most favourable when the higher education system is composed of a moderate number of medium-sized universities rather than very few large ones; or, indeed, a large number of tiny ones.

The gist of the argument is analogous to the mathematical truism that for any given series of numbers, the standard deviation from any number is least when that number is the mean of the series: eg in the series 1, 2, 3, 4, 5, the sum of the differences between a given number and any other number is least when the number is 3. Likewise, a minimum *overall* deviation from the optimum economies will occur when the scale is at the mean. The mean, in turn, may be defined by reference to the organization's objectives. Thus it is of the utmost importance to start by carefully defining these objectives, and then seeking to structure as efficiently as posible the *primary level* at which these objectives are pursued. Having defined the scale of this building-block, it becomes possible to design around it the supporting services and structures necessary to sustain it. Moreover, one finds oneself at a strategic vantage point from which one is able to further reduce TOTAL costs. This is possible by asking of each of the non-primary levels: are the resources (ie costs) deployed at each level completely and genuinely necessary for the fulfilment of the primary objectives? Experience in industry shows that, in practice, such an approach inevitably leads to a deeper understanding of the relationship between the various cost elements involved in producing and selling a product, and that total costs can be reduced by as much as 15% — 20% as a result. In the non-commercial environment of the university, such reductions can surely be emulated.

In proposing this methodology, one must reinforce the point that any financial economy only makes sense in so far as it results in a more efficient way of achieving the essential, stated objectives of the organization. It makes no sense at all if stringent economies result in the sacrifice of the objectives themselves. Any fool can cut costs: indeed the simplest way to secure the greatest savings is to close down altogether. But it takes a wiser man to achieve *real* efficiency: a slimmer, more virile, adaptive organization whose standards of excellence and impact on society are unimpaired.

THE RELATIONSHIP OF
THE CONCEPT OF ECONOMIES OF SCALE
TO THE ISSUES CONSIDERED BY THE
NATIONAL ADVISORY BODY
FOR LOCAL AUTHORITY HIGHER EDUCATION

Christopher Ball

The central concern of this chapter is to relate the theme of 'economies of scale in higher education' to the work of the National Advisory Body for Local Authority Higher Education (NAB) both in the short and in the longer term. It should be stated at the outset that the views put forward here are personal and do not seek to represent official policy of NAB.

There are a number of difficulties in addressing the issue of 'economies of scale' which it may be helpful to itemize in order to set them to one side. First of all, there is the question of prejudice; in commenting upon many subjects we are inevitably prejudiced — experience colours thinking. For my own part, for example, I approach the idea of economies of scale inevitably biased by experience in the Universities of Oxford and London (both very large institutions). Although such experience is modified to some extent through other activities, eg by acting as an external examiner for other universities, or by taking part in the validation of degree courses in the public sector, such second-hand experience hardly corrects sufficiently the primary experience of having served for a long time in two very large collegiate institutions. Others will have different experiences, and different prejudices. Secondly, there is the inevitable fact of conscious and unconscious loyalty to one's own institution, which makes it very difficult to recognize that it may not be as economic as it might be. All responsible and responsive institutions mitigate both the social and psychological disadvantages of great size and the financial disadvantages of small size; we can observe easily some of the ways in which this has happened over time. Such a statement begs the question, however, by assuming (as in some earlier chapters) that there are financial disadvantages from the one, and psychological and educational disadvantages from the other.

It may be self evident but it is surely true that human beings can in fact make most things work; they are extraordinarily adaptable, as is exemplified by higher education in this country, where people have achieved remarkable (although, perhaps, not very surprising) success in adapting institutions of very different sorts to carrying out a worthwhile job of higher education. It is difficult to think of a convincing example where it could be said that merely because of the size of an institution it is obviously a failure.

The third difficulty in contemplating the issue of economies of scale is the knowledge that to make changes to institutions is costly — not only does it cost money but it is also (often) very costly in human terms. There is nothing new in such a statement: we have all in the last few years watched (or had experience of) institutions being closed and merged in the teacher training rationalization process, and know something about the cost of making large scale changes to institutions. The universities are now experiencing something similar. We are, therefore, in general predisposed to try to avoid massive changes — which makes it difficult to contemplate the idea of economies of scale, since any decisive conclusions would almost inevitably involve substantial change. The cost of change is always an argument for inertia; whilst it may be a good argument it nevertheless inhibits consideration of the kind of issue which was put before the conference which gave rise to this book.

When trying to contemplate the issue in detail, it is important to clarify whether we are concerned to approach the problem on a *tabula rasa* basis, or to contemplate British higher education as it is, in all its awkward and interesting diversity. In approaching it on the *tabula rasa* basis one must recognize at the outset that economies of scale for an institution have to be approached first and foremost through defining the *role* of that institution. Is it a teaching or a research institution or, perhaps, a mixture of the two? The three possible answers here immediately lead to different views about economy of operation. Then, it is important to define the *level* of work offered by an institution of higher education — be it sub-degree, first degree, or postgraduate — and to note the tremendous variety and mixtures of levels available (notably) in the local authority sector including, most importantly, non-advanced further education. Having defined the level of work one should perhaps go on to define *mode* of study — full-time, sandwich, part-time or a mixture of these three; and then to define the *faculty range* of an institution. This latter point must be a decisive planning consideration; economies of scale will look very different once this question has been answered.

We are rarely however in a position to plan the whole of a new university or institution of higher education, let alone of planning a totally new system. Even when a new institution has been planned in this country (for example Keele University or the five later new English universities) the constraints of the prevalent model appear to have been very strong. There seems to be a pressure (either implicit or explicit) which encourages institutions to conform to the norm of size which operates across the system as a whole: the effect of the predominant model is extremely influential and should not be underestimated. The institution-wide desire to conform often leads to a failure to ask or answer questions of principle about organization and size.

Touching briefly on what has been described earlier as the appropriate size of management structures *at the system level*, I observe, first, that the question of how large and how extensive the higher education system as a whole should be in the United Kingdom was not (apparently) explicitly discussed at the conference. Despite this it may be useful to note, albeit briefly, the curious sectoral system of higher education in this country: there is one section constituted by the universities and funded by the UGC; there is a second (English) local authority sector (with NAB in its advisory capacity); and the DES with the voluntary colleges and direct grant institutions constitutes yet another sector, not to mention the Advisory Body for Local Authority Higher Education in Wales, the Scottish Education Department, and Northern Ireland. It is perhaps not unreasonable to question whether these are appropriate management structures at the system wide level!

Turning to that which is properly the concern of NAB, I note that some people have questioned whether it is actually possible to offer intelligent planning to a sector containing approximately four hundred institutions whilst retaining local education authority responsibility and control; the success (or otherwise) of the NAB will go some way to answering this question. A further question which has quite rightly been raised relates to whether the NAB and the UGC (representing the two major sectors of higher education) can co-operate intelligently to avoid the waste and overlap which is believed to occur at the local level (although the extent of wastage which occurs through failure to co-operate — or indeed to inform — across the binary line is not at all clear); these are important and critical questions but not, however, ones to which any answers are offered here.

Moving from the level of the system to that of the institution, one wonders whether it would be possible to achieve the ideal or optimum size of an institution — or for that matter of a department, or indeed a sector — assuming that the ideal size could be agreed upon. It is not reasonable to expect that anything of this nature can be done *in the short term*, but if there were a clear idea of what were the economies of scale, and the most cost effective as well as the most educationally, socially and psychologically effective size of an institution or department or sector, it might be possible to move towards this *over time*. It must be fairly obvious that if there were such a model, it would not be anything very precise — 4,000 full-time-equivalent (fte) students or something like that — and it would have to be a range. One such range has already been offered by Christian Schumacher with his idea of institutions of not less than 1,500 and not more than 4,000 students. Schumacher's paper made a very interesting contribution with a conclusion which, if accepted, would call into question the continued existence of a substantial number of large universities as well as polytechnics! If such a model were agreed, it would be an extremely important input to planners in terms of the basis upon which decisions are taken. But we would need to be very sure, however, about the virtues of such a model before proceeding to apply it as a sort of Procrustes Bed to British higher education. In approaching the problem of economies of scale many people must surely start from the essentially common sense position, supported by the Verry and Davies findings, that there are economies of scale in universities and that these are never exhausted, ie that average costs fall indefinitely as student numbers rise. Sear's paper (chapter 2) goes into these findings in much greater detail.

Such a view would seem to justify the large institutions — but not the small ones. Should the UGC and NAB make their decisions and give their advice to Government on this basis? It would seem at first glance to represent a coherent and sensible position as long as one could take account of the social and psychological problems (discussed in earlier chapters). An important counter to this argument, however, is that in the local authority sector of higher education, at least, — when one moves away from common sense and theory to practice or the reality of the situation — one is surprised to find that economies of scale operate to some degree in the opposite direction to theory. Local authority higher education to some extent has offered a picture of a reverse economy of scale: on a unit cost basis, some of the larger institutions are distinctly more expensive than the smaller ones. Looking at the universities it is also true that some large universities appear costly on a unit cost basis whereas some small universities appear to be operating very economically. The theory of economies of scale does not appear to correspond in any great degree with the realities of British higher education, and it is the realities with which we have to deal.

A further aspect of the reality of local authority higher education which cannot be ignored is the vitally important fact of non-advanced further education. In the sector for which NAB exercises responsibility, a large number of the four hundred or so institutions are mixed in the sense that they are engaged in both advanced (AFE) and non-advanced further education (NAFE) — and there are good educational arguments for having such institutions.

NAB is in difficulties here, however, in applying the concept of economies of scale since if applied from the point of view of AFE it will simply not impact sensibly upon the institution itself. Unlike the UGC, NAB is very often constitutionally concerned only with *parts* of an institution, ie the AFE part, which makes it extremely difficult to apply any crude measure of economies of scale to institutions overall. NAB must bear in mind constantly that economies of scale which might be desirable in terms of AFE could substantially affect important work in the NAFE sector.

In considering the short-term problem of readjusting the system to accommodate the cuts, NAB started from three principles which I would wish to defend very strongly, even though (as with any principles) there are costs involved. The first principle to be adopted was that in the planning exercise (for 1984/85) it was proper 'to ask institutions first' — ie to adopt a bottom-up approach. Although clearly the process has to be an iterative one, it is necessary to start somewhere and it was agreed that the best place to start was by asking the institutions what they thought should happen to them under certain resource constraints, which were fairly easy to define, and that NAB — in as much as it is the central planner — should take a second look and design a 'national plan' on the basis of institutions' own views and priorities. It would of course have been possible to do it the other way round — to design a 'national plan' to which institutions would have to accommodate themselves — but it was decided as a matter of principle to adopt the first approach and it is one which NAB would wish to defend. There are costs in such an approach: institutions have been asked to confront some very hard questions, but the important issue is whether (as I believe they do — and should) institutions really want to be able to govern themselves. Self-government involves responsibility for making hard decisions.

Secondly, NAB realized from the beginning, though the implications of this realization may still not be clearly understood by everybody, that it could not undertake its short-term exercise on a subject basis; it would have to be undertaken on an institutional basis. The recent UGC exercise typifies the subject based approach. The UGC reviewed subject provision through forty-four universities, and was able to do so because it had a developed sub-structure of subject boards, it knew the institutions well, there were only forty-four of them and there were experienced members of staff who had been in post at the UGC for a long time. In contrast, NAB started its life in February 1982 with no staff, no offices, no Working Groups and with only half the funds of the UGC. Even if it had been possible to develop a subject sub-structure in the time, the funds were not available to finance it. In addition the curriculum range in local authority higher education is wider than that in the university sector and would require a wider and much more complex subject sub-structure. Planning in the local authority sector, at least in the short term, has to be done on an institutional basis, and by making institutional decisions. The painful implications of an institutional approach should be clearly understood: any cuts which have to be made will be of institutions or parts of institutions. Unless NAB were to come to the conclusion that the right thing would be to apply an 'equal misery' cut at roughly ten per cent on every single institution (and it seems unlikely that this will be — or should be — the outcome), the inescapable logic of the two principles sketched out above demands and leads to a selective or discriminatory approach in the application of the overall cuts in resources.

The third principle concerns timing. NAB was brought into existence in February 1982 and was immediately faced with the challenge: could it impact in any real way on the 1983/84 pool allocation? There was never much chance of NAB being able to complete a detailed exercise by the autumn of 1982, which is when advice to the Secretary of State was required for the distribution of pool funds for 1983-4. The next real question therefore was whether or not the submission of advice to the Secretary of State should be left until 1984, to impact on the 1985/86 pool allocation. An inescapable conclusion in thinking about the latter time-scale was that the cuts would already have happened! In terms of the timing, NAB had very little choice — there was only one year left in which advice could sensibly be offered to the Secretary of State on the allocation of a reduced AFE pool. NAB has to give its advice by autumn 1983; this timescale was enforced not chosen. If it is thought that 1983 will be too early for NAB to be able to do anything more than rough justice to the system, the responsibility for this lies not primarily with NAB but rather with the timetable within which it is required to work.

What criteria can be applied in the very short time-scale outlined above? A number have loomed very large in the thinking within NAB and one of its tasks is to give priority to these criteria. The following section offers a personal attempt to order these priorities and will no doubt be different from those which other people might wish to put forward.

First, there is the question of regional distribution and the likely impact upon this of decisions within NAB for major institutional changes. There will be cases where the issue of regional distribution of higher education will override other criteria which might have led NAB to advise that pool funding be withdrawn from a specific institution. Any short-term rationalization of the sector must have due regard to this question. Secondly, there is the question of the national importance of work which is being offered within the sector. Is, for example, engineering more important to the nation than leisure studies? Certain things must follow in terms of NAB's short-term plan from the answer to such a question and it is a prime example of one of the key issues which must be tackled. Thirdly, there is the question of the impact of decisions about AFE on NAFE. Here NAB will need to depend on the advice of Regional Advisory Councils and HM Inspectorate on the interplay between AFE and NAFE. Fourth, there is quality. How is this going to be assessed? NAB is asking HMI and the validating bodies for advice and help, although it is not yet clear whether the validators will be able to give an appropriate answer. The criterion of quality comes relatively low down in my list of priorities largely because it is such a difficult indicator to measure; it is no use having a criterion if it cannot be applied. Fifth, and last, there is the question of cost effectiveness, and thus of economy of scale. It is interesting that the criterion which was the central theme of the conference should come at the bottom of the list but it should be emphasized that this relates to the implementation of the short-term as opposed to the long-term work of NAB.

There are of course other criteria which are perhaps as important as the five already listed, if not more so. There is, for example, the question of the maximum tolerable rate of change within institutions. Institutions can only be asked to change at a certain rate if they are to avoid destroying themselves or removing their effectiveness, and within higher education the rate of change is probably quite slow. Higher education institutions cannot change very fast and remain effective — the impact and constraint of a typical three year degree course is only one example here — and this relatively low maximum tolerable rate of change is a severe constraint which (perhaps) leads one to the conclusion that institutions should not be asked to change dramatically in the short term — rather they should continue relatively unaffected or disappear altogether.

The most urgent task which has faced NAB therefore is to advise on the implementation of a ten per cent reduction in the real level of resources available to local authority higher education, by the autumn of 1983. In so doing NAB must seek to determine how much of this reduction can legitimately come out of unit costs — ie how much 'fat' still exists in the system — and how much has to be achieved through excision of provision. The response from institutions to the short-term planning exercise is crucial in reaching a judgement between a squeeze on unit costs and excision of certain parts of the sector; it is, however, generally accepted that there will have to be a certain amount of amputation in the system, although the extent has yet to be determined. As already noted above, the interdependence between AFE and NAFE is such that a ten per cent reduction cannot (for example) be achieved by excising all the minor providers from the system. Neither, it should be remembered, are minor providers very costly; it is the major providers which are (often) less cost effective within the local authority system. This situation suggests that in order to achieve part of the ten per cent reduction, withdrawal of all AFE pool funding from one or more institutions may have to be recommended. In terms of a major provider this would obviously indicate closure of the institution. How should NAB's advice be framed? Should such an institution be closed? or merged with another, neighbouring institution? The traditional answer to such a dilemma has been that of merger, but is this, in the short term, the correct answer? Mergers create multi-site institutions which take some years to develop their own ethos and working relationships; they are, however, socially and politically more acceptable than outright closure and it may be that for these reasons the advice from NAB will lean towards this kind of solution. Whatever the solution, it will lead to cessation of work and this will inevitably raise the question of redundancies; money cannot be saved without saving on staff. This is a critical issue which needs to be faced squarely.

Equally, however, all the solutions must also, it is suggested, raise the question of the control of student numbers. Can the local authority sector for much longer continue to be the part of higher education which has no effective control over student numbers? There are no effective means at present for controlling them, but whatever means are found will not contribute to economies of scale! It must be clear that economies of scale, as a concept, is not really helpful to the short-term task facing NAB. It may be more useful in the longer term but much more research is needed, not least to show why the theory of economies of scale and the facts of British higher education do not always correspond. We need to understand the pressures which have caused the growth of big institutions in the last twenty years before we can plan for smaller units, if that is what the social and psychological arguments point to. It is undoubtedly true that more research is needed, but this is for the longer rather than the shorter term. As far as the NAB is concerned, at least in the short term, getting decisions taken at the right time is the most important thing.

ISSUES, RESEARCH, ACTION

Sinclair Goodlad

This chapter reviews some of the major issues identified by those who took part in the joint Higher Education Foundation/Department of Education and Science conference; highlights some of the topics on which further research is needed; and suggests a few considerations which could usefully inform future action in the planning of institutions of different sizes. Although what is written draws heavily on the collective and individual views of participants, I must take responsibility for the views expressed. In particular, I stress that they do not necessarily represent the views either of the Trustees of the Higher Education Foundation or of the Department of Education and Science.

SOME MAJOR ISSUES EMERGING FROM THE CONSULTATION

The Conflict Between the Economic and Sociological/Psychological Analyses of Economies of Scale

The economists argue that financial economies increase more or less indefinitely with every increase in the size of institutions of higher education, although there are some indications that in the public sector some of the largest institutions have the highest unit costs. By contrast, many sociologists and psychologists (some of whose research is reviewed above by Thomas and Chickering) suggest that large institutions have a damaging effect on the morale and motivation of individuals who may perceive themselves to be socially redundant. For example, in large institutions, a smaller proportion of students actively participate in activities than in small institutions; the activities of those who do participate become less varied and more specialized; students of marginal ability are left out, ignored, or denied the opportunity to participate; peer evaluation shifts from criterion referenced (how suited to the job) to norm referenced (how good compared to others); hierarchies of prestige and power develop; rules of conduct, and the definition of appropriate behaviour, become increasingly formalized and rigid. All of these factors have effects on students' sense of involvement with their colleges and, in consequence, on their efficiency and effectiveness in studying. At present, because these effects cannot be quantified, they are left out of economists' cost-benefit analyses.

The Conflict between Centralization and Institutional Autonomy

At times of financial retrenchment, there is political pressure for centralized planning of the higher education system as a whole, so that unnecessary duplication of work can be avoided. A national plan is not, however, compatible with devolved decision-making. Similarly, at the level of individual institutions, participative management (which involves having many decision points, with consequent pluralism) is not compatible with firm institutional priorities and purposes. Much discussion revolved around the relative attractions of small institutions (perhaps geographically convenient, facilitating part-time study, mobilizing community support, providing a sense of involvement for staff and students) and large ones (having more political 'crunch' and thereby, perhaps, being better able to secure their survival in a national plan). The conflict is ultimately that between peer management (which is usually discipline-based) and government management (which, while seeking to secure an appropriate balance of subjects nationally, is necessarily institution based). While peer management may tolerate, even encourage, a multiplicity of institutional forms, perhaps with federal sharing of desirable facilities, government management may set more store on limiting the number of institutions with which it has to negotiate — thereby favouring large aggregations rather than small ones.

Should Institutions Specialize in Teaching or Research?

Again to achieve financial savings, it may appear politically attractive to concentrate research funding on to specific institutions ('centres of excellence') or to pay lecturers separately for their teaching and research. These ideas were, however, resisted by the consultation on the grounds that: 'research' has a wide range of meanings and cannot in any case be disentangled from 'teaching' (eg 'teaching' research students); research budgets would seem more of a luxury and be more liable to be axed if visibly separate from teaching budgets; individuals capable of and interested in doing research who did not happen to be in favoured institutions must be given the sense of hope that stems from knowing that anyone can apply for research funds; at departmental level, there can be a very wide range of combinations of teaching, research, and administration. Good teachers are perhaps retained by the knowledge that they can do (are, indeed, expected to do) research — whether or not (as is hotly disputed) teaching and research ability are related. Christopher Ball drew an analogy with further education, in which excellent NAFE sometimes rides on the back of poor AFE: which is what attracts the good staff (the 'piggy-back' principle). In short, the opinion seemed to be that questions concerning the differential funding of teaching and research can, and should, be separated from those of institutional size.

The Possibility of Greater Permeability of Institutional Boundaries

One of the undoubted attractions of very large higher education institutions, particularly if loosely articulated internally, is flexibility. Martin Trow emphasizes the need for 'slack' in budgets, with the possibility of funds being moved from one area to another to stimulate and nourish new ideas: institutions, he urged, need 'lots of rocks for little furry creatures to hide in'. The danger, of course, is that the furry creatures might be dozing — that 'slack' becomes identified with slacking. There seemed to be no easy answer on how to ensure that everyone is working hard. It is, however, possible to think of achieving greater budgetary flexibility while maintaining the collegial effectiveness of relatively small institutions.

There are already examples of small institutions sharing expensive library or computing facilities, financial and personnel administrators, and credit transfer arrangements (to permit students to move freely between institutions to build up a degree course). The key conceptual difference may be that between *aggregation* (to which we in the United Kingdom may be overly attached) and *federation* (used, for example, by a group of private and state institutions in the San Francisco Bay area of California).

Relating Size to Management Objectives: Using Informed Judgement

There was a preference widely expressed in the consultation for the exercise of informed judgement over the use of objective, quantitative criteria in reaching management decisions. Many things easy to measure are not very valuable, and many valuable things are not easy to measure. In most cases, purpose should determine size. At the University of California, Berkeley, for example, class sizes can range from 3 to 900 — depending upon what they are doing. The overall staff/student ratio used for a degree course as a whole may be crucial; but within the degree judgements have to be made about the costs and educational benefits of each type of activity.

Political decisions about higher education nearly always demand informed judgement — which has to go beyond what is quantifiable. For example it may seem unthinkable to ask for 'slack' in budgets when the preoccupation of politicians is to cut budgets and to devise fail-safe mechanisms to avoid extravagance. Yet, as Halsey and Trow (1971, p. 169), among others, demonstrate, the quest for reputation is a dominating academic motivation which, although not quantifiable, may lead to a very effective use of whatever resources are available.

Again, it is politically necessary to justify higher education over against the need for hospitals, roads, geriatric care, and other expensive social needs. What value is attached to a period of time in higher education can vary between individuals: in the United Kingdom the word 'wastage' is used to describe students who leave higher education without taking a qualification, yet in the United States no stigma attaches to leaving a course — two years in college is believed to have value whether or not a qualification is achieved.

SOME ISSUES ON WHICH RESEARCH IS NEEDED

Data on Financial Economies

Hard data are badly needed on purely financial economies sought and achieved by various administrative arrangements. For example, as Kevin Sear urges in chapter 2 above, much information is needed on the utilization of buildings.

Case Studies

There are abundant opportunities, as there is singular need, for case studies of mergers and closures to yield information on how decisions are actually arrived at and what their effects are. The National Advisory Body has established some research on the effects of its own activity. It would be valuable if all institutions kept abundant administrative intelligence in a form accessible to researchers and/or published accounts of how they went about their work.

It may be difficult to institute the study of adjustment to financial cuts in mid-stream; but subsequent analysis of how institutions respond to the external determination of their size should yield fascinating insights into how issues of scale have been (or have not been) high in the priorities of internal and external negotiation. The future analysis, and understanding, of educational administration will be aided by thoughtful record-keeping now.

Relationship between Quality and Size

The possible relationship between the quality and size of institutions and departments would be worth testing. This would be an extremely complex type of study to conduct — not least because correlation does not imply causation. The real value of attempting such a study might be to sharpen our perception of what is meant by 'quality'. Close observation, after the manner of 'educational anthropology' or ecology, might be more suitable than broad econometric or psychometric study for this type of research.

Normative Constructs

A rich seam of potential research material lies in the normative constructs of the DES and LEAs concerning institutional size. Eric Briault's discussion paper (which has not been reprinted here for lack of space) demonstrated the richness of the material concerning school size; similar study relating to the planning of higher and further education would be very illuminating.

Value Systems

As re-organization of educational institutions is proposed — in the interest of economies of scale or simply to cut cash costs by closures — most of us in educational institutions offer elaborate and subtle defences of our activity. What we write, and say, should provide future researchers with illuminating material about the value systems we use. If more effort is put into revealing these values (as, indeed, this book is seeking to do), our decision-making should be made more sensitive and effective.

SOME FACTORS WHICH SHOULD INFLUENCE THE PLANNING OF HIGHER EDUCATION PROVISION

As Christopher Ball's paper (chapter 8 above) has forcefully demonstrated, decisions about the planning of provision for higher education are rarely made on a *tabula rasa* basis, and are often (as with the work of the NAB) made under considerable political pressures of time and money. Although most people adapt and adjust remarkably well to whatever institutional arrangements they find themselves in, there are undoubtedly stresses and strains, endemic in some forms of organization, which might be eased by attention to the root causes. These stresses and strains might include, as the chapters of this book have indicated: anomic feelings of students in large and impersonal institutions; feelings of alienation, restriction, closed opportunities of students in very small ones; lack of commitment by staff and students to institutions which are too complex or amorphous or geographically scattered to evoke loyalty; a sense of frustration among staff at the lack of facilities or of irritation among administrators at under-use or inefficient use of facilities; rigidity of control over curricula from inadequate or inappropriate channels of communication between teachers and validators.

Logically, one cannot derive intentions from a study of effects, although obviously one's judgement about what it is sensible to attempt will be influenced by what one expects to achieve. It is, therefore, useful to try (as this book tries) to separate out the economic, administrative, social, psychological, and other consequences of different types of arrangement for teaching and research. Perhaps the most useful outcome of the exercise is the renewed perception that objectives can be achieved in several different ways. For example, federation, as indicated above (page 82) may be more effective in some circumstances than aggregation. Institutions and functions may be considered independently, and individuals can be assigned functions under any one of a variety of institutional arrangements. Functions of higher education might include, *inter alia*: research (concept formation, data gathering, etc.); scholarship (the refinement of observation, interpretation, evaluation); consultancy (dissemination of ideas to action agencies); teaching (creating the conditions for learning and the assessment of achievement); social development (fostering interpersonal skills and competencies, widening of intellectual horizons among students); social service (provision of action of direct social utility by staff and students); transmission of culture (stimulus, at local or national level, of 'high' culture by provision of theatres, concert halls, art galleries) etc. At present, these functions are distributed with considerable variation among different types of social institution. When funds are limited, our first instinct is to think of institutions rather than functions, because institutions are the means whereby the functions are carried out and, to put it crudely, from which we are paid. What the analysis of economies of scale in higher education fruitfully suggests, however, is not so much ways of making institutions cheaper (although this clearly is one possible effect to be achieved), but rather alternative ways of distributing functions between individuals. As interactions between individuals become regular and patterned, so new 'institutions' emerge which may or may not achieve administrative visibility and continuity. A preference for *aggregation* implies cramming as many functions as possible under one administrative umbrella; a preference for *federation* implies first identifying the functions, then establishing whatever dispositions of individuals' time and activity is most effective both in cash terms and in terms of the job-satisfaction of the individual.

To achieve an effective mix of functions, an individual may need to move between different types of institution, not *seriatim* (at different periods of the individual's career), but rather simultaneously — by membership of or affiliation to several institutions rather than one. This already occurs when, for example, a polytechnic lecturer does research at a neighbouring university, or when a university research student does some school teaching, or an industrial research and development specialist gives seminars in an institution of higher education. At the conference, Maurice Kogan suggested that marginality may, in fact, make for more effective work, in that the marginal person may put more effort and thought into what is not a full-time activity: the university teacher may be a good consultant, just as the professional consultant may be good at teaching.

It is a commonplace of sociological analysis of modern industrial societies that the spread of rationality has been closely associated with the increased and more specialized division of labour in society. As systematic thought has been applied to social action, tasks (both intellectual and manual) have been broken down into ever smaller pieces in the interests of efficiency. What we are now realizing is that we are rapidly losing sight of the overall picture (the sense of direction, meaning, purpose) as this process accelerates. The more we set up specific institutional arrangements to administer specialized tasks, the more rigid (and often less efficient) do our social arrangements seem to become.

In higher education, each of the functions listed above has achieved its own institutional embodiment with associated mechanisms of funding. When funding is cut, the 'institutions' (the administrative embodiments of the functions) are forced into competition with each other so that we seem to have to make unpalatable choices between desirable ends. What some of the analysis offered in the chapters of this book, however, suggests is that there may be considerable redundancy at the individual level simply as an effect of institutional arrangements. It is not that the capability of the individual is not *needed*; rather it is that institutional arrangements do not permit that capability to be *exercised*. Economy of scale at one level of the system (as Christian Schumacher so clearly demonstrates in chapter 7) may lead to diseconomy at another level. If the 'federation' approach were to be more vigorously espoused, it might be possible to evolve new administrative structures more capable than existing ones of identifying the functions of which each individual was capable and permitting a much more fluid movement of individuals between institutions in carrying out those functions. With the present (understandable) defensiveness about existing institutions, some people are made redundant (and given nothing at all to do) while others are worked to the point of collapse. The discussion about the concept of economies of scale in higher education, although it may not have produced immediate proposals for reform, did at least suggest some factors which should influence the planning of higher education provision if maximum flexibility of deployment of individuals in institutions is to be achieved. The considerations listed below are not intended as a definitive, nor the most important, classification of possibilities: they are perhaps the most obvious and easily realizable.

Appointment of Staff to an Area

One major (although sometimes under-publicized) reason for mergers may be the need to move staff about, ie to secure specific functions but with different individuals. Small institutions are undoubtedly less flexible than big ones for this purpose. Administrative flexibility could be increased (with perhaps great savings in the stress on individuals) if individual members of staff were appointed to an *area* with a group of institutions (possibly including universities, polytechnics, institutes of higher education, further education colleges, and schools) in the anticipation that the individual would work in a combination of locations. Rather than becoming redundant as the demand for work by specific institutions fluctuated, the individual could simply be assigned a new combination of functions. It is probable that individuals would experience considerable continuity of work in specific locations (with the many 'collegial' benefits thereby offered). However, appointment to an area, rather than to the payroll of a specific institution, might make for greater security.

Increased Sharing of Facilities

Already, the sharing of expensive facilities by a cluster of institutions seems to work well in some places. If the primary functions of individuals, and of institutions, are separated from the support functions, very considerable flexibility of arrangement can be contemplated. Highly fluid groupings of individuals whose primary functions were teaching, research, consultancy, etc. could be supported by central facilities such as libraries, computing, personnel, and accountancy facilities. Electronic data handling makes this type of redistribution of functions (which previously depended heavily on files of paper in specific locations) much easier to contemplate than even ten years ago.

The primary functions of support services can, of course, (as already happens very widely) be complemented by secondary functions. For example, halls of residence in institutions of higher education double as conference centres and hotels; computing services, television production facilities, laboratory services, etc. are 'marketed' to non-academic organizations.

With suitably flexible arrangements of this sort, new courses could be set up quickly without, for example, a specific institution having to demonstrate to a validating body that the institution's own library held an adequate range of materials; it would be sufficient to demonstrate that the materials were readily available to students in a given area. Similarly, individual lecturers or groups of lecturers could get research grants by demonstrating that they had access to suitable research facilities not necessarily within one location (at present their employing institution) but in an area consisting of several colleges which shared facilities.

The analysis of economies of scale points up the paradox that our institutional arrangements need to be simultaneously both 'bigger' and 'smaller'. That is to say, for the flexibility described above one might envisage small groups of individuals based at particular colleges drawing upon the full range of support facilities of a very big area. Once the intention (or management objective) is clearly defined, and provided that sufficiently flexible arrangements are achieved, enormous possibilities open up. Such arrangements would also secure the sound management principle of maximizing the accountability of each administrative sub-unit.

Multiple Functions for Academic Staff

The obvious corollary of the possible appointment of staff to an area and of the increased sharing of facilities is the need for academic staff to have a multiplicity of functions. To say this is to say nothing new: already academic staff have many independent and interlocking functions — which is what makes academic work so immensely rewarding. What is needed is perhaps more systematic exploration of the possibilities of these functions being exercised not only across departmental or other basic unit boundaries, but also across institutional boundaries. It might, then, become usual, rather than exceptional, for an individual to teach at two separate institutions; or teach at one and do research at another; or work in industry and take postgraduate seminars at a university; etc. What is difficult is to achieve not only an entrepreneurial ethos among academic staff (that is there already), but also administrative arrangements which steer an appropriate path between accountability and control. On the one hand it is reasonable that academics should give value for money to their employers; but this must not be secured at the cost of snarling everyone up in complex conditions of employment (hours of work per day/month/year etc.) which can generate a clock-watching mentality and limit the time needed for unaccounted reflection, for creative disturbance of routine, for the serendipity effect of unstructured mingling with colleagues.

Administrative initiatives (as contrasted with those of individual academics, which already abound) might consist of removing all possible barriers to free and flexible movement of people, funds, resources. Administrative measures might include adjusting pension rules; modifying fte (full-time student equivalent) calculations to facilitate inter-departmental or inter-institutional activity; opening libraries to anyone who cared to use them (and tracking users electronically for retrospective audit and subsequent planning of provision); reviewing pay and promotion criteria to accommodate teaching, consultancy, community service as well as international visibility in research; and so on.

Mobility, Residence, and Part-time Study
Just as there may be merit in academic staff having multiple functions, so there may be advantages in students doing so. The Open University has demonstrated the attractions to mature students of part-time study combined with a job with which to provide for one's family. Plans for the number and size of academic institutions need to take account of the possibilities of students moving about for part-time study. As Kevin Sear indicates, the cost of residence is a significant factor in the overall costs of education; similarly, the cost (and time-inconvenience) of travel is to be reckoned. Broadcast radio and television, disc and cassette sound and video recordings, correspondence courses and self-study packages do not remove the need for face-to-face teaching, for which a wide geographical disposition of relatively small teaching institutions may be more desirable than aggregation into very large ones.

It is impossible to make general prescriptions about these matters; suffice it to note that mobility, residence (full time or part time), and part-time study must all be added to the equation concerning economies of scale.

Provision of a Firm Collegial Base
Against the suggestions offered in the previous three sections (aimed at achieving greater freedom and flexibility in higher education — with the associated probable economies of scale) must be balanced the need to offer both students and staff a firm collegial base. As chapter 6 reveals, there is abundant evidence of the effect on students' satisfaction with college and on their achievement of a sense of belonging. The collegial base which offers this sense of belonging may be an actual college, as with Oxbridge colleges or small monotechnic institutions (cf. Gay 1979; Wyatt 1977a and 1977b); but it can equally well be a department. The sense of 'collegiality' seems to depend on the experience of energy directed towards a common goal; on regular, unstructured interactions with colleagues; on shared experiences. In actual colleges, these can readily be achieved by participation in sports; by residence; by college functions such as concerts, plays, etc.; and even by the shared experience of regularly eating bad food together in uncomfortable if venerable surroundings. To create the experience of 'collegiality' in non-collegial settings may require more conscious planning, but is not too difficult to achieve.

Conviviality, the root of collegiality, can be stimulated by both academic and non-academic activity. The most fruitful form of energy directed towards a common goal is, perhaps, the academic one of shared research, teaching, or community service. Undergraduate research opportunities, which (as at the Massachusetts Institute of Technology) encourage undergraduates to assist with the research of the staff to the mutual benefit of both staff and students, offer many opportunities for informal interaction. So too do field trips, group projects, studio or laboratory work, or most contexts for learning which require interpersonal transactions as part of the process of study. Academic staff may well need specific training (through staff development courses) to handle such situations effectively.

Collegiate rituals, to take a Durkheimian position, may be valuable primarily because individuals assemble to celebrate them and thereby have the opportunity for interpersonal contact, the feeling of belonging, and so forth. Ceremonies involving incantations in Latin and gyrations in gowns and mortar boards may nowadays lack appeal to both academic staff and to students. There are, however, abundant opportunities for less formal academic rituals. Like religious rituals, these may well centre upon rites of passage: departmental celebrations of outside honours; welcoming of new members (both staff and student); retirements or promotions; exhibitions of degree or diploma projects; inaugural lectures by those promoted to chairs; special lectures by visitors; colloquia by academic staff or by students on their project work; publication parties for new books; in short, any or every occasion for signifying recognition of one another's contribution to the life of the collegial base — section, department, school, or whatever — can and should be seized upon. In view of the evidence of the effects on purely academic work of the sense of belonging, it is not sentimentally nostalgic to suggest that attention needs to be given to making collegial occasions as pleasant as possible so that staff and students positively enjoy them rather than find them a chore.

It might, perhaps, be added that there is a distinct economic benefit to be derived from establishing for students some such firm collegial base. As Oxbridge colleges and American universities have known for years, and as convocations of other British universities are now discovering, the loyalty of alumni can result in many and various benefactions both in cash and in kind. If notions like those sketched in the three sections (pp. 86 — 87) above are adopted, the real challenge will be to establish the experience of 'collegiality' for part-time students, taught by part-time staff, in buildings which serve as, perhaps, school, adult education and community centre, and teaching facility for university, polytechnic, or further education college.

The Devolution of Curriculum Decisions
A severe diseconomy can occur if students are not able to learn what academic staff feel best equipped to teach. There are many indications that detailed decisions about the curriculum are best handled at basic unit level (cf. Becher and Kogan 1980, chapter 6). This is not to deny the value and importance of peer review of some sort, but rather to suggest that in this area (as in many others) short lines of administrative control are best, in which assessors (external examiners, validators, and others) can have detailed knowledge of the content of the curriculum and of teaching methods. Large institutions, with big senate or board of studies meetings, may lose the intimacy of contact with teachers and knowledge of detail which makes decisions valuable. Time can be wasted and innovation stifled if people act as curriculum validators who cannot possibly know the operating requirements of the teachers.

Negotiative Patterns of Governance
To achieve a sensible balance of the factors that seem to make for economies of scale in higher education it may be necessary to establish negotiative patterns of governance. External factors (such as financial accountability and strategic control of the balance of subjects locally and nationally) require well-informed, strong centralist intervention; internal factors (such as detailed supervision of the curriculum, the provision of adequate collegial bases) require the wisdom of detailed local knowledge. It is unlikely that any individual or corporate agency will have adequately detailed knowledge in all these areas. Negotiative governance does not, however, imply that the partners have equal *power*: those who give resources have more power. Rather, the overall efficiency and effectiveness (as contrasted with financial cheapness) of higher education requires compromises. The chapters of this book will, we hope, have indicated the range of issues which need to be considered when these compromises are negotiated. We did not find — and were not expecting to find — any formula which would enable us to balance the quantifiable factors against the unquantifiable, the cost against the benefit. We hope, however, that we may have started the process of establishing a climate of opinion, a context of shared assumptions, against which piecemeal reforms may be planned and evaluated.

APPENDIX A

Authors: *Economies of Scale in Higher Education*

CHRISTOPHER BALL is Warden of Keble College, Oxford, and Chairman of the National Advisory Body. He was Lecturer in Comparative Linguistics at the School of Oriental and African Studies, University of London, 1961-64, and Fellow and Tutor in English Language, Lincoln College, Oxford, 1964-1979. From 1973 to 1980 he was Chairman of the Council for National Academic Awards English Studies Board.

MARK BLAUG has been a Professor at the University of London Institute of Education since 1967. He was Assistant Professor of Economics at Yale University for nine years before becoming a Reader at London University. His publications include *Causes of Graduate Unemployment in India* (1970), *An Introduction to the Economics of Education* (1971), and *A Plain Man's Guide to the Finance of British Higher Education* (1980).

ARTHUR CHICKERING is Distinguished Professor of Higher Education and Director of the Center for the Study of Higher Education at Memphis State University, Tennessee. During 1970-71, he was a visiting scholar at the Office of Research at the American Council on Education. From 1971 to 1977, he played a major role in creating Empire State College as vice-president for academic affairs. His major publications include *Education and Identity* (1969), *Commuting versus Resident Students* (1974), *Experience and Learning* (1977), and *Developing the College Curriculum* (with W. Bergquist, D. Halliburton, and J. Lindquist) (1977). He is editor of *The Modern American College* (1981).

SINCLAIR GOODLAD is Senior Lecturer in the Presentation of Technical Information at the Imperial College of Science & Technology, London University, and Honorary Secretary of the Higher Education Foundation. He has taught at Delhi University and at the Massachusetts Institute of Technology. His publications include *Conflict and Consensus in Higher Education* (1976), and *Learning by Teaching* (1979), and he was editor of and contributor to *Education and Social Action* (1975), *Project Methods in Higher Education* (1975), and *Study Service* (1982).

CHRISTIAN SCHUMACHER has spent most of his working life in the steel industry as a corporate strategist and in personnel management. In 1979 he left the steel industry to become the Seear Industrial Fellow at the London School of Economics, a post which he held until 1981, when he set up his own private consultancy company engaged in restructuring and reorganizing industrial and other institutions. He is a member of the Industrial Panel of the British Council of Churches and a Trustee of the Higher Education Foundation.

KEVIN SEAR is an Economic Adviser working in the Economics Division at the Department of Education and Science. He joined the Department in 1976, and has been involved in the study of a wide range of topics including analysis of local authority expenditure and calculation of the education Grant Related Expenditure figures which are used in the determination of local authority block grant. He has also been a member of the Department's Financial Modelling Team. Currently he is engaged on various policy issues in higher education. He has written his chapter in a personal capacity; the views expressed in it are not necessarily those of the Department of Education and Science.

RUSSELL THOMAS is an Associate Professor in Counseling and Personnel Services and a staff member in the Center for the Study of Higher Education, College of Education, Memphis State University, Tennessee. He has taught for several years at Ohio University and Memphis State University in the general area of counselling and college student personnel, specializing in individual appraisal and college student development. He has published papers on such topics as mentoring, values education, and cognitive/learning styles.

MARTIN TROW is Director of the Center for Studies in Higher Education, University of California, Berkeley. He is well known in the United Kingdom as a scholar in the comparative study of higher education systems and as co-author (with A.H. Halsey) of *The British Academics* (1971).

GORDON WHEELER is Director of the Further Education Staff College, Coombe Lodge. He has held department headships at Slough College of Higher Education and at Hendon and Bournemouth, and has worked in local authority finance services at Luton. He has been Chairman of the Education Committee of the Institution of Industrial Managers. He has published widely on educational matters and acted as an adviser on industrial and educational management in Jamaica, Hong Kong, Singapore, and Malaysia.

APPENDIX B

Participants: Joint HEF/DES Conference October 1982

* Dr. C. Ball	Keble College, Oxford
Professor A. Becher	University of Sussex
Dr. E. Briault	Formerly ILEA
* Professor A. Chickering	Memphis State University, USA
Mr. J. Crawford	Birmingham LEA
Dr. C. Cullingford	Oxford Polytechnic
Mr. B. Cullen	DES
Professor J.C. Dancy	University of Exeter (Chairman)
Dr. J. Gay	Culham College Institute
* Dr. J.S.R. Goodlad	Imperial College, London
Dr. D. Harrison	Keele University
Mr. S.R.C. Jones	City of London Polytechnic
Dr. E. Kerr	Council for National Academic Awards
Professor K. Keohane	Roehampton Institute of Higher Education
Professor M. Kogan	Brunel University
Dr. H. Law	Portsmouth Polytechnic
Mr. M. Le Guillou	HMI, DES
Mr. P. Levasseur	INHE Programme, OECD
Dr. J. May	Derby Lonsdale College of Higher Education
Mrs. Pauline Perry	HMI, DES
* Mr. C. Schumacher	Independent Consultant
* Mr. K.J. Sear	DES
Mr. J.H. Thompson	DES
* Professor M. Trow	University of California, Berkeley
* Mr. G. Wheeler	The Further Education Staff College
Mr. J.F. Wyatt	West Sussex Institute of Higher Education
Mrs. Ann King	DES (Secretary)

*Authors of chapters

APPENDIX C

Trustees: The Higher Education Foundation

APPENDIX D

The Higher Education Foundation

The Higher Education Foundation is a charitable body whose purpose is to analyse and understand the fundamental values and objectives of higher education. It was formed in 1980 by amalgamation of the Foundation for the Study of Values in Higher Education and the longer-standing Higher Education Group.

The Higher Education Foundation is not concerned with propaganda for a preconceived theory or belief. In particular, though many of its supporters are Christians, many also are not, and its value position would more properly be described as Christian-compatible than as Christian in any exclusive sense.

The Chairman has summarized its stance in four points:

1 We share with all forms of liberal humanism a deep concern for *scholarship*, for the advancement of learning by research and teaching.

2 Nevertheless of ultimate concern are *persons*. And we see persons not just as thinking but as feeling and choosing, so we aim at a balance between objectivity and commitment.

3 We also see persons not just as individuals but as inescapably *social*. Higher education has a responsibility to society at large. This responsibility is exercised not just by service, ie by meeting the expressed needs of society, but also from time to time by challenge and criticism.

4 Finally, our perspective implies a special kind of *realism* about human affairs and institutions. In Lewis Mumford's words, we can "accept limitation, uncertainty and eventual death as necessary attributes of life ... and as the conditions for achieving wholeness, autonomy and creativity."

It will be seen that running through these four points is the theme of balance. That is why the position of the Foundation may shift in order to correct contemporary imbalances. What matters is, first, that questions of value are not ignored and, secondly, that some reasonable balance is maintained when it comes to the answers which issue in policy.

The Foundation operates in various modes. Its regular *Consultations* tackle issues in higher education which both cause current concern and spring from or lead to deeper value questions. Consultations already held or planned are:

1981   Study Service
       Validation
1982   Reductionism in Psychology, Biology and Medicine
       Business Values and Undergraduate Business Studies Courses
       Economies of Scale in Higher Education.

Consultations bring together an invited group of people competent and engaged in the area concerned. They seek to explore the underlying philosophical issues, to identify areas for research, and to suggest action. Their findings usually lead to *publications*. They may also be taken further at the open *Annual Conference*, a successful feature of the Higher Education Group taken over by the Higher Education Foundation. All these operations are overseen by the Trustees, who also from time to time offer *Research Fellowships*, particularly for the preparation of consultations.

The Foundation welcomes individual members. An annual subscription of £5, which may be covenanted, entitles subscribers to the Newsletter issued twice a year and the opportunity of participating in the Annual Conference, normally held in the spring. Applications to the Assistant Secretary, Peter Spicer, at Salt Mill House, Mill Lane, Chichester PO19 3JN.

TRUSTEES AND SUPPORTERS

Registered Charity No. 281719

REFERENCES

Astin, A.W. (1963) Differential college effects on the motivation of talented students to obtain the PhD *Journal of Educational Psychology* 54 (1), 63-71

Astin, A.W. (1977) *Four Critical Years: Effects of College on Beliefs, Attitudes, and Knowledge* Jossey-Bass, San Francisco

Barker, R.G. and Gump, P.V. (1964) *Big School, Small School* Stanford University Press, Stanford, California

Bayer, A.E. (1975) Faculty Composition, Institutional Structure, and Students' College Environment *Journal of Higher Education* 46 (5), 549 - 555

Beal, P.E. and Noel, L. (1980) *What Works in Student Retention* American College Testing Program

Becher, A. and Kogan, M. (1980) *Process and Structure in Higher Education* Heinemann, London

Bereday, G.Z.F. (1973) *Universities for All* Jossey-Bass, San Francisco

Bernstein, A.R. (1976) How big is too big? In Vermilye, D.W. (ed.) *Individualizing the System* Jossey-Bass, San Francisco

Blaug, M. (1980) *A Plain Man's Guide to the Finance of British Higher Education* University of Stanford Institute for Research on Educational Finance, Stanford, California

Blaug, M. (1981) The Economic Costs and Benefits of Overseas Students, In Williams, P. (ed.) *The Overseas Student Question: Studies for a Policy* Heinemann, London

Bottomley, J. et al. (1972) *Costs and Potential Economies* O.E.C.D., Paris

Bowen, H.R. (1977) *Investment in Learning: The Individual and Social Value of American Higher Education* Jossey-Bass, San Francisco

Brawer, F.B. (1973) *New Perspectives on Personality Development in College Students* Jossey-Bass, San Francisco

Carnegie Commission (1973) *Priorities for Action:* The Final Report of the Carnegie Commission on Higher Education, New York

Chickering, A.W. (1969) *Education and Identity* Jossey-Bass, San Francisco

Chickering, A.W. (1971) The Best Colleges have the Least Effect *Saturday Review* 16 January 1971

Chickering, A.W. et. al. (1981) *The Modern American College* Jossey-Bass, San Francisco

David, M. (1976) Size and education in a chimerical relationship *New Universities Quarterly* 31. Winter 1976/77, 73 - 108

Davis, J. (1964) *Great Aspirations: The Graduate School Plans of America's College Seniors* Aldine, Chicago

Dewey, J. (1938) *Democracy and Education* Macmillan, New York

Dunworth, J. and Cook, R. (1976) Budgetary Devolution as an Aid to University Efficiency *Higher Education* 5, 153 - 167

Eddy, E.G. Jr. (1959) The College Influence on Student Character *American Council on Education*

Erikson, E.H. (1950) Growth and Crisis of the 'Healthy Personality' in Senn, M.J.E. (ed.) *Symposium on the Healthy Personality* Supplement II. 91 - 146. Josiah Macy Jr. Foundation, New York

Feldman, K.A. and Newcomb, T.M. (1969) *The Impact of College on Students* Jossey-Bass, San Francisco

Festinger, L. (1957) *A Theory of Cognitive Dissonance* Row, Peterson, New York

Gaff, J.G. et al. (1969) *The Cluster College* Jossey-Bass, San Francisco

Gallant, J.A. and Prothero, J.W. (1972) Weight-Watching at the University: The Consequences of Growth *Science* 28 January 1972, 175, 381 - 388

Gay, J.D. (1979) *The Christian Campus?* Culham College Institute, Abingdon

Halsey, A.H. and Trow, M.A. (1971) *The British Academics* Faber and Faber, London

Hare, A.P. (1962) *Handbook of Small Group Research* Free Press, Glencoe, Illinois

Heath, D.H. (1981) A College's Ethos: A Neglected Key to Effectiveness and Survival *Liberal Education* 67, 89 - 111

Heider, F. (1958) *The Psychology of Interpersonal Relations* Wiley, New York

Helson, H. (1964) *Adaptation-level Theory* Harper, New York

Isaac, J.F. (1977) Studies in Educational Change: Towards a Theory of the Middle Ground. PhD Thesis, University of Birmingham

Jacob, P.E. (1957) *Changing Values in College* Harper, New York

Katz, J. and Associates (1968) *No Time for Youth* Jossey-Bass, San Francisco

Klemp, G.O. Jr. (1977) Three Factors of Success, In Vermilye, D.W. (ed.) *Relating Work and Education* Jossey-Bass, San Francisco

Layard, R. and Verry, D. (1975) Cost Functions for University Teaching and Research *Economic Journal* 85 (337) 55 - 74

Lumsden, K.G. (1978) *New Technologies in Higher Education* Esmee Fairbairn Research Centre, Heriot-Watt University

McNamara, D.R. and Ross, A.M. (1982) *The B.Ed. Degree and Its Future* Report on the Initial Teacher Training Project sponsored by the Department of Education and Science at the University of Lancaster (1977-1981). School of Education, University of Lancaster

Miller, E. and Rice, A. (1967) *Systems of Organization* Tavistock, London

Newcomb, T.M. (1943) *Personality and Social Change* Dryden Press, New York

Newcomb, T.M., Koenig, K., Flacks, R. and Warwick, D.P. (1967) *Persistence and Change: Bennington College and its students after twenty-five years* Wiley, New York

Newton, D., Shaw, K.E., and Wormald, E. (1975) *Change in Colleges of Education* ATCDE Occasional Papers on Sociology of Education 2

Oldham, G. (ed.) (1982) *The Future of Research* Leverhulme Programme of Study into the Future of Higher Education. SRHE Monograph 47, Society for Research into Higher Education, Guildford, Surrey

Pascarella, E.T. (1980) Student-Faculty Informal Contact and College Outcomes *Review of Educational Research* 50 Winter, 545 - 595

Raushenbush, E. (1964) *The Student and his Studies* Wesleyan University, Middletown, Connecticut

Rogers, C.R. (1961) *On Becoming a Person* Houghton Mifflin, Boston

Sale, K. (1982) *Human Scale* Perigree, New York

Sanford, N. (1962) The Developmental Status of Entering Freshmen in Sanford, N. (ed.) *The American College* Wiley, New York. 253 - 282

Sanford, N. (1966) *Self and Society: Social Change and Individual Development* Atherton Press, New York

Schumacher, E.F. (1973) *Small is Beautiful: Economics As If People Mattered* Harper and Row, New York

Shaw, K.E. (1978) Contractions and mergers of United Kingdom Colleges of Education: some logistic comments *The Journal of Educational Administration* XVI. 2. 212 - 218

Smith, M.B. (1966) Explorations in Competence: A Study of Peace Corps Teachers in Ghana *American Psychologist* 21 (6) 555 - 566

Smith, V.B. and Bernstein, A. R. (1979) *The Impersonal Campus* Jossey-Bass, San Francisco

Solomon, L.C. and Taubman, P.J. (1973) *Does College Matter? Some Evidence on the Impacts of Higher Education* Academic Press, New York

Thistlewaite, D.L. (1960) College Press and Changes in Study Plans of Talented Students *Journal of Educational Psychology* 51 (4), 222 - 233

Verry, D. and Davies, B. (1976) *University Costs and Output* Elsevier Scientific Publishing Company Ltd.

Wallace, W.L. (1966) *Student Culture* Aldine, Chicago

Winter, D., McClelland, D.C., and Stewart, A.J. (1981) *A New Case for the Liberal Arts* Jossey-Bass, San Francisco

Work Research Unit (1978) *Occasional Paper No.10.* Department of Employment, London

Wyatt, J.F. (1977a) The Idea of Community in Institutions of Higher Education *Studies in Higher Education* 125-135

Wyatt, J.F. (1977b) 'Collegiality' during a Period of Rapid Change in Higher Education: An Examination of a Distinctive Feature Claimed by a Group of Colleges of Education in the 1960s and 1970s *Oxford Review of Education* 147 - 155

DEMCO